The Real Reasons for Seasons— Sun-Earth Connections:

~ Unraveling Misconceptions About the Earth and Sun ~

Grades 6–8

Skills

Observing, Inferring, Graphing, Analyzing Data, Designing and Making Models, Visualizing, Drawing Conclusions, Explaining, Communicating

Concepts

Causes of the Seasons, Sun-Earth Connection, Spherical Earth, Earth's Orbit and Rotation, Ellipse, Tilt of the Earth, Northern and Southern Hemispheres, Latitude and Longitude, Temperature, Angle of Sunlight

Themes

Models and Simulations, Systems and Interactions, Patterns of Change, Scale, Stability, Diversity and Unity

Mathematics Strands

Number, Measurement, Geometry, Logic and Language

Nature of Science and Mathematics

Changing Nature of Facts and Theories, Interdisciplinary, Real-Life Applications

by

Alan Gould, Carolyn Willard, *and* Stephen Pompea

LHS GEMS

Great Explorations in Math and Science
Lawrence Hall of Science
University of California at Berkeley

Lawrence Hall of Science

Cover Design
Lisa Baker

Design and Illustrations
Alan Gould
Lisa Baker

Photographs
Richard Hoyt
Laurence Bradley
Alan Gould

Lawrence Hall of Science, University of California,
Berkeley, CA 94720-5200

Director: Ian Carmichael

Support for the development of this GEMS Guide was provided by the NASA Office of Space Science through cooperative agreement #NCC5-253 to the Sun-Earth Connection Education Forum, UC Berkeley Space Sciences Laboratory. We greatly appreciate this support!

Initial support for the origination and publication of the GEMS series was provided by the A.W. Mellon Foundation and the Carnegie Corporation of New York. Under a grant from the National Science Foundation, GEMS Leader's Workshops have been held across the country. GEMS has also received support from: the McDonnell-Douglas Foundation and the McDonnell-Douglas Employee's Community Fund; Employees Community Fund of Boeing California and the Boeing Corporation; the Hewlett Packard Company; the people at Chevron USA; the William K. Holt Foundation; Join Hands, the Health and Safety Educational Alliance; the Microscopy Society of America (MSA); the Shell Oil Company Foundation; the Crail-Johnson Foundation; and the NASA Sun-Earth Connection Education Forum. GEMS also gratefully acknowledges the contribution of word processing equipment from Apple Computer, Inc. This support does not imply responsibility for statements or views expressed in publications of the GEMS program. For further information on GEMS leadership opportunities, or to receive a catalog and the *GEMS Network News*, please contact GEMS at the address and phone number below. We also welcome letters to the *GEMS Network News*.

International Standard Book Number: 0-924886-45-5

COMMENTS WELCOME !

Great Explorations in Math and Science (GEMS) is an ongoing curriculum development project. GEMS guides are revised periodically, to incorporate teacher comments and new approaches. We welcome your criticisms, suggestions, helpful hints, and any anecdotes about your experience presenting GEMS activities. Your suggestions will be reviewed each time a GEMS guide is revised. Please send your comments to: GEMS Revisions, c/o Lawrence Hall of Science, University of California, Berkeley, CA 94720-5200. The phone number is (510) 642-7771 and the fax number is (510) 643-0309. You can also reach us by e-mail at gems@uclink4.berkeley.edu or visit our web site at lawrencehallofscience.org/GEMS

Great Explorations in Math and Science (GEMS) Program

LHS GEMS

The Lawrence Hall of Science (LHS) is a public science center on the University of California at Berkeley campus. LHS offers a full program of activities for the public, including workshops and classes, exhibits, films, lectures, and special events. LHS is also a center for teacher education and curriculum research and development.

Over the years, LHS staff have developed a multitude of activities, assembly programs, classes, and interactive exhibits. These programs have proven to be successful at the Hall and should be useful to schools, other science centers, museums, and community groups. A number of these guided-discovery activities have been published under the Great Explorations in Math and Science (GEMS) title, after an extensive refinement and adaptation process that includes classroom testing of trial versions, modifications to ensure the use of easy-to-obtain materials, with carefully written and edited step-by-step instructions and background information to allow presentation by teachers without special background in mathematics or science.

Staff

Director: Jacqueline Barber
Associate Director: Kimi Hosoume
Associate Director/Principal Editor: Lincoln Bergman
Mathematics Curriculum Specialist: Jaine Kopp
GEMS Network Director: Carolyn Willard
GEMS Workshop Coordinator: Laura Tucker
Staff Development Specialists: Lynn Barakos, Katharine Barrett, Kevin Beals, Ellen Blinderman, Gigi Dornfest, John Erickson, Stan Fukunaga, Philip Gonsalves, Linda Lipner, Karen Ostlund, Debra Sutter
Distribution Coordinator: Karen Milligan
Workshop Administrator: Terry Cort
Financial Assistant: Vivian Tong
Distribution Representative: Felicia Roston
Shipping Assistant: Maureen Johnson
Director of Marketing and Promotion: Matthew Osborn
Senior Editor: Carl Babcock
Editor: Florence Stone
Principal Publications Coordinator: Kay Fairwell
Art Director: Lisa Haderlie Baker
Senior Artists: Carol Bevilacqua, Rose Craig, Lisa Klofkorn
Staff Assistants: Carilee Lutnick, Thania Sanchez, Dareyn Stilwell, Stacey Touson, Jennifer Yee

Contributing Authors

Jacqueline Barber
Katharine Barrett
Kevin Beals
Lincoln Bergman
Susan Brady
Beverly Braxton
Kevin Cuff
Linda De Lucchi
Gigi Dornfest

Jean Echols
John Erickson
Philip Gonsalves
Jan M. Goodman
Alan Gould
Catherine Halversen
Kimi Hosoume
Susan Jagoda
Jaine Kopp

Linda Lipner
Larry Malone
Cary I. Sneider
Craig Strang
Debra Sutter
Herbert Thier
Jennifer Meux White
Carolyn Willard

Reviewers

We would like to thank the following educators who reviewed, tested, or coordinated the reviewing of this GEMS guide. Their critical comments and recommendations, based on classroom presentation of these activities nationwide, contributed significantly to this publication. A number of teachers in the second round of testing also helped review the CD, and three additional teachers (also listed below) focused on CD review. Participation in this review process does not necessarily imply endorsement of the GEMS program or responsibility for statements or views expressed. Their role is an invaluable one; feedback is carefully recorded and integrated as appropriate into the publications.

ALASKA

Verstovia Elementary School, Sitka
Jackie DiGennaro*
Jan Love
Carolyn Mork
Vonnie Franceschini
Kay McCarthy

CALIFORNIA

Park Middle School, Antioch
Ruth   Becky
Paula McEvoy
Debi Molina *
Sandy Weigand

Martin Luther King Middle School, Berkeley
Jennifer Brouhard
Jay Cohen
Lynn Pacunas
Beth Sonnenberg*
Phoebe Tanner

Castro Elementary School, El Cerrito
Jim Aiken*
Leethel Farmer
Steve Monson,
Kelly Terry

Warwick Elementary School, Fremont
Pardis Baradar
Jan Elyo
Katy Johnson
M. Nishyama
Ann Trammel*
M. Wells

Thank You!

Livingston Middle School, Livingston
Sue Campbell*
Heather Cardoso
Bill Grunloh
Howla Jardali
Filomena Sousa

Arts School, Oakland
Bill Compton
Jae Agu

Hillcrest Elementary School, Oakland
Suzy Garren
Ann Iverson
Caroline Yee*

Edendale Middle School, San Lorenzo
Kristen Can
Rebecca Davis*
Molly Goldsmith
Abby McAllister
Sue Niec

* Trial test coordinator

FLORIDA

Howard Middle School, Orlando
Amy Arnold
Elaine Aikens
Tehani Padilla
Susan Leeds*

OHIO

Hannah Gibbons, Cleveland
Bill Badders*
Gary Saunders
Andrea Rice
Tara Stringfellow

Drake Planetarium, Norwood
Pam Bowers*
Paige Gipson
Nancy Moorman
John Stoddard
Val Stacy

WISCONSIN

St. John Lutheran, Milwaukee
Dave Allerheiligen*
Rita Allerheiligen
Craig Hirschman
Henry Meyer

Additional CD reviewers:

Warren G. Barta, Cheyenne Mountain High School,
    Colorado Springs, Colorado
Regina Biros, Kellogg School, Chicago, Illinois
Jeffery A. Yuhas, Reading Memorial High School,
    Reading, Massachusetts

CD-ROM Development Team

Stephen M. Pompea, Pompea & Associates, Lead CD-ROM Author
Alan Gould, LHS, CD-ROM Author, Lead GEMS guide author
DC Spensley, SSL. Lead CD-ROM Design, GUI & Information Design
Igor Ruderman, SSL, Lead CD Programmer
Diane Kisich, SSL, Project Manager
Isabel Hawkins, SSL, Co-Director NASA's Sun-Earth Connection Education Forum
Lincoln Bergman, LHS GEMS Principal Editor

Recommended Computer Requirements for Your CD-ROM!

PC:
Hardware
Pentium 100
4X CD-ROM
Operating System: Windows 95, 98, 2000, or Windows NT 4.0
Memory: Windows 95/98: 32 MB RAM (64 recommended).
NT 4.0 and Windows 2000: 64 MB RAM (128 recommended).

Software (included on CD-ROM)
Acrobat 4.0 or higher
QuickTime 3.0 or higher
Netscape 3.0 or higher or Internet Explorer 4.0 or higher

Macintosh
Hardware
Power Mac with OS8 or higher operating system
4X CD-ROM
Memory: 32 MB RAM

Software (included on CD-ROM)
Acrobat 4.0 or higher
QuickTime 3.0 or higher
Netscape 3.0 or higher or Internet Explorer 4.0 or higher

Please note: The recommended monitor resolution setting for viewing the CD-ROM is 800 x 600 pixels (or higher).

Acknowledgments

The authors must first acknowledge Dr. Isabel Hawkins, Senior Fellow, Research Astronomer, and Director for Science Education at the Space Sciences Laboratory (SSL) of the University of California at Berkeley. This book owes a great deal to Isabel's vision, leadership, expertise, and devotion to education. She brought together the authors and other staff and consultants from GEMS and SSL, took part in numerous brainstorming and planning sessions, observed several pilot and local trial classroom presentations of the activities, read and advised at all stages of development, and marshaled the resources for both the guide and the CD-ROM—the first-ever CD in the GEMS series. To Isabel—astronomical thanks! Thanks as well to Diane Kisich, Igor Ruderman, DC Spensley, Karen Meyer, Brionna Garner, and others affiliated with SSL who assisted inmany ways with this guide and CD. Jacqueline Barber, Director of the GEMS program and LHS Associate Director, also played an important role in helping frame and define the major learning goals in light of national standards and research on student misconceptions.

We would also like to thank Dr. Cary I. Sneider, former GEMS Science Curriculum Specialist, now at the Boston Museum of Science. Cary's work in astronomy education is deservedly famous and he is the author of many GEMS guides, including *Oobleck* and *Earth, Moon, and Stars*. Cary was part of the initial discussions that led to the selection of this seasons-related topic, and was kind enough to review the national trial version of the guide.

The guide was also reviewed by Dr. Sten Odenwald, a well-known research astronomer and educator, who is Education and Public Outreach Manager for the IMAGE satellite project and also connected with the NASA Sun-Earth Connection Education Forum. Sten is the author of *The Astronomy Café*, which is both a book and an internet resource (see the "Resources" section for more details).

We would also like to acknowledge the Project Universe/Annenberg program for their groundbreaking work in the area of student misconceptions about the seasons (we highly recommend the "Private Universe" video listed in the "Resources"). We adapted the idea of a survey from one that appears on their web site at http://www.learner.org/teacherslab/pup/surveys.html

We gathered and adapted much of the data that students analyze in this unit from the Global Learning and Observations to Benefit the Environment (GLOBE) program, a worldwide network of students, teachers, and scientists working together to study and understand the global environment. Their website can be found at http://www.globe.gov/

The teachers who tested these activities and/or helped us test the CD are listed at the front of the guide. We would especially like to thank David Glaser, whose classroom at Willard Middle School in Berkeley was the proving ground for the earliest version of these activities. And we'd like to thank the students and their parents at LHS astronomy summer camps for their willingness to appear in photographs in this guide and in several short movies on the CD.

Contents

Please Note: *The Real Reasons for Seasons: Sun-Earth Connections* makes an excellent extension and/or follow-up to the GEMS guide *Earth, Moon, and Stars.* In particular, the first two sessions of *Earth, Moon, and Stars* deal with concepts that are a prerequisite to understanding seasons, including the spherical Earth, the Earth's rotation, and the Earth's revolution around the Sun.

Developed with funding from the NASA Sun-Earth Connection Education Forum (SECEF)

This GEMS Teacher Guide comes with a CD-ROM with a wealth of supporting resources: articles, stories, images, movies, web links, and powerful software. Two software packages are included on the CD-ROM:

• *Seasons* (by Riverside Scientific, Inc.) enables the exploration of the causes of seasons by viewing cycles of temperature, daily solar energy, and hours of daylight, with adjustment tools to change the Earth's axis tilt and the Earth's orbit shape.

• *Starry Night* (by SiennaSoftware, now Space.com), a powerful planetarium program, can be used to determine where the Sun, Moon, and stars are at any date. It is very useful in general in teaching about astronomy and can be used to create movies showing the position of the Sun at different times of the year from different locations.

Introduction

In *The Real Reasons for Seasons: Sun-Earth Connections* unit, students are guided systematically toward an understanding of what causes our planet's seasons. Many students and adults have misconceptions about the causes of seasons. We often need to reflect on and discard some of our familiar old concepts about the Sun-Earth relationship before we can understand the "real reasons behind the seasons." This process of revising models or explanations is at the heart of science. In this unit, students must think like scientists as they constantly challenge and revise their own ideas in the same way that scientists do.

Research done by Philip M. Sadler, at the Harvard-Smithsonian Center for Astrophysics, found that understanding the causes of seasons is challenging for people of all ages. The video, *A Private Universe*, which was one result of Dr. Sadler's research, shows that even Harvard graduates are hard-pressed to answer the question, "What causes the seasons?" The articulate graduates interviewed in the video *think* they know the causes of seasons, and speak confidently, but most of them have mistaken ideas. They, like most adults, do seem to fully understand the following concepts, all of which are prerequisite to understanding what causes seasons:

- The Earth is spherical.
- The Earth spins (rotates once every 24 hours), which causes day and night.
- The Earth orbits (revolves) around the Sun once a year.

In fact, many of us harbor misconceptions related to the above concepts that send us down the wrong track when thinking about the causes of the seasons. Our misconceptions often involve creative—even ingenious—but incorrect explanations. Many of us hold onto and embellish our erroneous personal explanations for the seasons throughout all the years of school, and we become very good at fitting new information into our old, comfortable private models. Our students often do the same. They arrive in class with their own frameworks and preconceptions, sometimes also called alternate conceptions.

> "Every time we communicate new concepts, we compete with the preconceived ideas of our listeners. All students hold these ideas but are unaware of their private theories. We must make them aware. Only then can we enable them to learn and free them from this private universe." (from the video *A Private Universe*)

Extensive research about how students best acquire a number of key science concepts has been done (and continues). This research must examine the alternate conceptions that students bring into the classroom and the kinds of instruction needed for students to modify

One excellent and very accessible book on student conceptual understanding in science is Children's Ideas in Science, *edited by R. Driver, E. Guesne, and A. Tiberghien, Open University Press, Milton Keynes Publishers, 1985.*

those ideas so they are more accurate. Such studies show that students (of all ages) do not abandon their ideas easily—after all, they have constructed their ideas over time, based on their experience and learning—it makes sense that changes in those ideas also take time.

So it is important to understand that no one single experience is likely to move all of your students from their initial conceptions to a full and accurate understanding. The questionnaire in this unit, and your assessments of student understanding throughout the activities, will provide insight into your students' progress. But even though this unit was specifically designed to grapple with common student misconceptions about the causes of the seasons, it is highly likely that some students may continue to have difficulty, and that even those who may seem to understand may still harbor less accurate ideas and theories. **Understanding of a complex topic such as this one has to be seen as taking place along a continuum—this unit seeks to bring all of your students further along that continuum and you can definitely count yourself successful—a teacher for all seasons!—if you have done that!**

Research also indicates that one of the best ways to get people to correct their misconceptions is to provide them with revealing experiences and allow time for them to compare and discuss alternative ideas/explanations so they themselves discover the flaws in their own thinking. In the case of topics, such as the causes for the Earth's seasons, which are known to be particularly difficult to fully grasp, it is highly likely that a variety of educational experiences over time— including hands-on or other interactive activities that cause students to confront their current ideas, modeling activities that help students visualize phenomena, analysis of new data that raises questions about their initial ideas, group discussions and debates—will all be important to helping students put together their revised and more scientifically correct understanding of the interrelationship between the Sun and the Earth that accounts for what we know as the Earth's seasons. Providing a mix of these experiences is what we have tried to do in this unit.

What *Are* Some Common Misconceptions About Seasons?

There are several common misconceptions about what causes seasons. Some of these have to do with the distance between the Earth and Sun. When asked, "What causes the seasons?" many people say, "When the Earth is closer to the Sun, we have summer; when the Earth is farther from the Sun, we have winter." This response can indicate many things, but upon probing, we may find the person has some of the following ideas:

- Many people think that the Earth's orbit around the Sun is a skinny (elongated) ellipse, causing Earth's distance from the Sun to vary dramatically at different points.

- Many think that the Sun is "off-center" within our orbit, again causing Earth to be closer or farther away from the Sun at different times.

- Some people know that the Earth's tilt has something to do with the seasons, and they think that the tilt makes us significantly closer to the Sun at certain times of the year.

What's wrong with those ideas?

- The Earth's orbit is indeed elliptical, but it is not at all "skinny." It is very nearly a perfect circle.

- True, the Sun is at one focus of Earth's elliptical orbit, but the orbit is so nearly circular that the Earth-Sun distance remains very nearly constant throughout the year.

- The tilt of the Earth is a key factor, but the tilt does **not** make any significant difference in the **distance** to the Sun. Because the distance from the Earth to the Sun is so enormous, the difference in distance caused by the tilt is not significant. This scale is important to understand: Imagine a pinhead Earth and a beach ball Sun about 30 meters apart. It does not make much difference in the distance between them if the pinhead tilts a bit!

> *The actual Earth-Sun distance varies between about 147,000,000 to 151,000,000 km. This difference of about 4 million km (not quite 3%) is not significant compared to the overall distance.*

If it's not distance, what DOES cause the seasons?

1. The Earth spins on its north-south axis, and the spin axis is tilted so that the North Pole points at the North Star all the time. As the Earth revolves around the Sun, the northern hemisphere is tilted toward the Sun at some times of the year (A) and away from the Sun at the other part of the year (B).

2. When the Northern Hemisphere is tilted toward the Sun, it has summer because:

   a. There are more hours of daylight.

   b. Sunlight strikes the Northern Hemisphere at a higher angle (more perpendicular), making the sunlight more concentrated, and resulting in more heating.

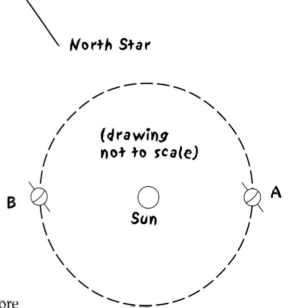

Unfortunately, simply explaining seasons, as many textbooks do, is not enough. Students need to unravel their current misconceptions if they are to fully understand this important concept. The eight activities described in this book are designed to do just that.

How this Unit Addresses Common Misconceptions and Gets at the Real Reasons for Seasons— An Overview of the Eight Main Activities

The *Seasons: A Sun-Earth Connection* unit is a series of activities designed to challenge common misconceptions. For example, the idea that Earth's distance from the Sun causes the seasons is first thrown into doubt when students prove to themselves in Activity 4 that the Earth's orbit is circular, and later when they discover, in Activities 6 and 7, that opposite seasons happen simultaneously in the northern and southern hemispheres. The real causes of the seasons are finally revealed in Activities 8 and 9.

Activity 1, "Name the Season," is a science writing activity in which students write paragraphs depicting scenes or events that have recognizable season-related elements, but without mentioning an actual season name. Students read each other's paragraphs and try to identify which season the author is describing.

In the "Sun-Earth Survey" (Activity 2), students answer some questions about seasons. Their responses will give you an idea of their current understanding of seasons and related concepts. For homework, each student surveys two friends or family members using the same survey. In the second part of the activity, after graphing the class data from all surveys, students draw conclusions about their own and others' general ideas about seasons. Most of the subsequent activities refer back to this survey, in a deepening re-examination of concepts, and to help students construct their revised ideas.

In the first steps of an imaginary "Trip to the Sun" (Activity 3), students monitor their altitude above Earth while they are traveling directly towards the Sun in a straight line at sunrise (starting out with the Sun on the horizon). The fact that their altitude above the Earth is increasing is because of the round shape of the Earth. Towards the end of the trip, students examine close-up images of the Sun. Not only will students enjoy this imaginary trip, but they will gain a better understanding of the spherical Earth and its size in relation to its distance from the Sun. Both of these concepts will help students in later sessions as they develop their understanding of the causes of the seasons. At the end of this Activity, the class sets up a scale model of the trip and finds that distance to the Sun is very large compared with the size of the Earth.

Students discover in "What Shape Is Earth's Orbit?" (Activity 4) that the true shape of the Earth's orbit around the Sun is very nearly a perfect circle. This begins to dispel misconceptions that seasons are caused by variation in Sun-Earth distance.

In "Temperatures Around the World" (Activity 5), students analyze temperature data taken from the Globe project, an Internet-mediated system of schools around the world dedicated to providing scientifically valid data on environmental characteristics related to weather, climate, and ecology. In graphing the data, students discover interesting relationships in temperature changes—that the pattern of temperature change from summer to winter in one hemisphere is reversed with respect to the opposite hemisphere. This further dispels the idea that the Earth-Sun distance is responsible for seasons.

Students find a similar mirror pattern in "Days and Nights Around the World" (Activity 6). They graph and analyze number of hours of daylight from cities around the world.

Students create a model of the Sun-Earth system in "Tilted Earth" (Activity 7) to arrive at the best explanation for what causes seasons. In "The Angle of Sunlight/Seasons Unraveled" (Activity 8), students see how the concentration of sunlight striking the ground is affected by the angle at which the sunlight hits the ground. In closure, students return to the survey, discuss the entire unit, and summarize the various elements they have found that help explain the causes of seasons.

Student written materials are arranged so that you may create for each student a "Seasons Lab Book." Masters for the 16 pages of the Seasons Lab Book are at the end of this guide.

Sections on resources, assessment of student learning, literature connections, and summary outlines for convenience in classroom presentation are included in this book. There are also numerous related resources, web sites, and software on the CD-ROM. See the next page for a text introduction to the CD. Throughout the unit, at points where the CD may be of use or special interest, we'll call your attention to it by placing our suggestions in the "Get Out Your CD-ROM" box as seen on the next page.

We are well aware that not all teachers and classrooms have access to computers or the internet. The activities in the guide do not depend on such access and the entire unit can and has been presented very successfully based solely on the instructions and activities in the printed guide. We intended that to be the case. At the same time, the CD can greatly enrich the unit, and has been designed to closely connect with as well as extend each of the main activities. We are very interested in whether and how you use it, and we welcome criticisms, suggestions, and a description of your approach to it (one computer in the classroom as a station, many computers, a computer with projection, a computer lab, other arrangements?). Was the CD helpful to you? To your students? In what ways? How do you plan to use it in the future?

Send us comments via email, letter, or phone. We consider them each time a guide is revised. If your letter is published in the *GEMS Network News*, you can receive a free GEMS guide of your choice. And now, on to "the real reasons for seasons!"

Please see the bottom of page 5 for "Recommended Computer Requirements for Your CD-ROM."

Get Out Your CD-ROM!

Introduction to the CD-ROM

The material on the CD-ROM designed for use with this unit is meant to support the print guide and in that sense is considered an integral part of the unit. It is for the use of teachers, as well as students. Although you may teach this unit successfully without this technological component, the learning experience and educational impact are considerably enhanced by using elements on the CD-ROM in conjunction with the activities in the teacher's guide. The CD-ROM contains images, selections from software, video clips, web pages, and web references to support the print guide. Each section of this print guide has boxes, like this one, describing how to use the CD-ROM. The best way to use the CD-ROM is to have it loaded on your computer as you go through the print guide. The CD-ROM has reinforcing material and may be particularly useful to teachers and students who are visual learners.

The CD-ROM has different kinds of materials on it, organized around the activities of the printed GEMS Guide.

Videos and Simulations
You can watch the Earth rotate, or see if Greenland is lit by the Sun in the winter. You can also take a trip around the solar system.

Slide Shows
We have several packaged slide shows on the latest research on the Sun.

Software
We have packaged Starry Night, a powerful planetarium program that can be used to determine where the Sun, Moon, and stars are at any date. Starry Night is produced by **Sienna Software**, and is used with permission. We also have permission to use simulation software on the seasons—in a time-limited version from **Riverside Scientific**—that allows you to experiment with seasons by changing the Earth's tilt or its orbit. Can Minnesota be made warmer than Florida by changing the Earth's tilt?

Web Pages
Many useful web pages about seasons and other Sun-Earth connections have been captured for easy access. Lessons and web pages were developed with teachers and have been tested in schools across the country.

Images and Data Sets
We have images of the Sun taken at solar observatories, to support student experiments and "Going Further" activities.

Supplemental Material
We have also included material on planned NASA missions that may appeal to your students, such as a NASA probe that will actually attempt to go to the Sun.

See page 5 for "Recommended Computer Requirements for Your CD-ROM"

Time Frame

Depending on your schedule, the age and experience of your students, and your teaching style, you may want to plan on combining two of the shorter activities in the same class period. This would work especially well if you have block scheduling or a self-contained class. Please understand that the time frames estimated below are based on a nmber of presentations in diverse classrooms, but are only estimates. Classroom activity and discussion time will vary, depending on your own unique situation.

Activity 1: Name the Season .... 30–45 minutes

Activity 2: Sun-Earth Survey.. 30–45 minutes
            Results of the Survey .... 30–45 minutes

Activity 3: Trip to the Sun .... 45–90 minutes

Activity 4: What Shape Is Earth's Orbit? .... 30–45 minutes

Activity 5: Temperatures Around the World .... 45–90 minutes

Activity 6: Days and Nights Around the World .... 45 minutes

Activity 7: Tilted Earth .... 45 minutes

Activity 8: The Angle of Sunlight/Seasons Unraveled .... 45 minutes

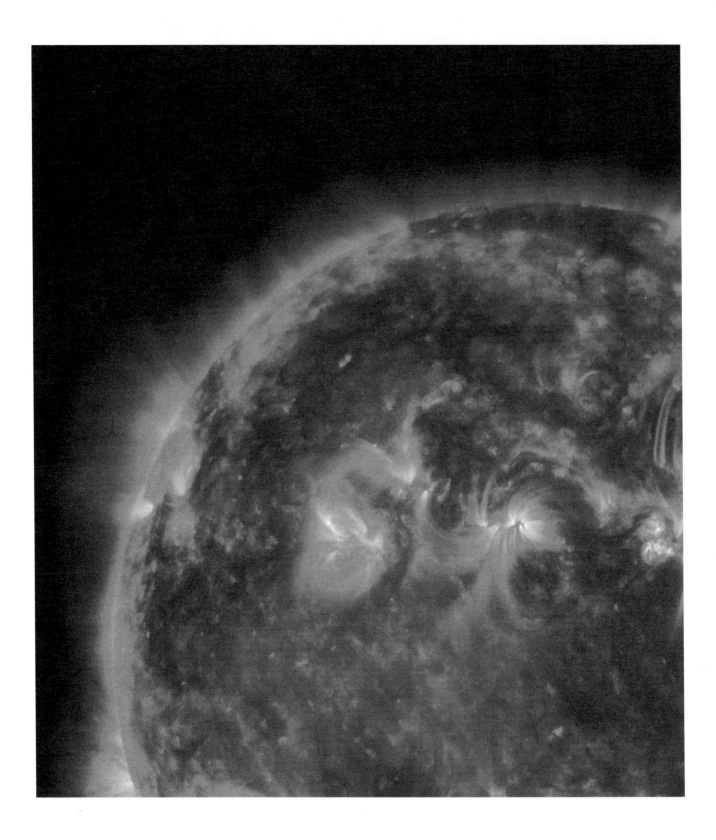

The Real Reasons for Seasons

Activity 1: Name the Season

Overview

In this first short activity, your students focus on their own experiences with seasonal change. Students write paragraphs depicting scenes or events that have recognizable season-related elements, but that do not mention an actual season name. They then play a game in which everyone tries to identify which season their classmates are describing.

This activity will probably take only part of a class period, and helps set the stage for learning about why seasons occur.

What You Need

For each student:
- ❏ 1 sheet of writing paper
- ❏ 1 Seasons Lab Book (or just the "Seasons Game" sheet, page 3 of Seasons Lab Book)
- ❏ 1 pencil

For the class:
- ❏ a chalkboard or overhead projector
- ❏ *Optional*—some sort of prize for the winner of the Seasons Game, e.g., decorative pen or pencil, a computer diskette, paperback book.

Getting Ready

Photocopy the entire *Seasons Lab Book* for each student at this time. This will save you some preparation time in future sessions. *Optional*: Fill in all the students' names on page 3 of the *Seasons Lab Book* before photocopying. This will save time by students not struggling with how to spell each other's names.

Introducing Seasons

1. Introduce this unit by telling the class they will be studying a number of relationships between the Earth and the Sun, and in particular what causes seasons.

2. Ask, "What kinds of changes occur with the seasons?" Accept a variety of answers, jotting them down on the chalkboard or overhead projector. [it gets hotter, colder, flowers bloom, baseball season opens, etc.]

> *One teacher we know started out this unit with a riddle. She said to the class. "OK . . . I've got a riddle. Sara's mother had four children. Their names were summer, fall, winter, and . . . what was the fourth one named? (there was a chorus of "spring!" . . . no said the teacher . . . the fourth one's name was Sara! Remember, I said Sara's mother . . . "*
> *Following a pause for groans . . she then added, "But if we were talking about summer, fall, winter, spring, what would we be talking about? That's right . . . the seasons!"*

3. Point out that the changes they have listed can be organized into some general categories: **biological changes** (plants, animals), **meteorological changes** (weather), **sociological changes** (events, celebrations, holidays, clothing).

4. Create a quick reference chart of seasonal changes by listing the four seasons vertically along the left edge of the chalkboard, and writing "Biological, Meteorological, and Sociological" across the top of the chalkboard. (You may prefer to use different categories, such as Life, Weather, Holidays, Sports Events, School Events.) Have students help you put some of the changes they've listed into the appropriate spots on the chart. Elicit additional events and changes typical of each season, until you have at least a few listed in each category of the chart. Leave the chart up for the rest of this class session.

	Biological (Life Changes)	Meteorological (Weather Changes)	Sociological: Holidays	Sports Events	School Events
Fall					
Winter					
Spring					
Summer					

5. Say that they now get to play a game called "Name the Season." Mention that they can use the chart to help them play.

6. Give each student a Seasons Lab Book. Have them write their names on the covers and turn to the Seasons Game Rules on page 3. Go over the rules together:

a. Pick one season to write about. On a piece of paper, write your name, but *not* the name of the season.

b. Write a paragraph describing some events, and include clues about what season it is. Without actually naming the season, make it possible for the reader to figure out what season it is.

c. At a "Ready-Set-Go" signal, leave your paragraph on your desk, and pick up a pencil and your Seasons Lab Book. Walk around and read as many of the paragraphs as possible, guessing what season each refers to.

d. For each paragraph, write on the "Seasons Game" sheet (page 3 in the Lab Book) the name of the person who wrote it and which season you think is being described.

e. The person with the most correct guesses wins the game.

Get Out Your CD-ROM!

Seasons and Civilizations Just as seasons cause significant changes in the weather, longer-term climatic fluctuations such as El Niño have affected civilizations. Read about how El Niño may have affected a sixth century civilization in Peru in an excerpt from a book that appears on the CD-ROM. Just go to the CD Home screen and click on the item under Activity 1: *Seasons and Civiliations*.

7. Give a few examples of how to use seasonal clues, asking if students can guess the season:

• Aah! aah! aah! aah choo! I have been sneezing all day because of all the plant pollens. But I love playing outside because it is not cold or raining. My dog is shedding.

• Everyday I feel like I'm melting. Kids playing sports are really sweating. Lots of people are in line at the ice cream shop. My sister and I squirted cool water at each other with squirt guns. The Sun will stay up until eight o'clock, and then fireworks!

• Today me and my friend took a walk and saw many different colored leaves. When I got home my mom made me rake up the leaves that fell on our lawn. When I put them in a pile, I jumped in!

• I was freezing cold. When I went to sleep, I put extra blankets over me. In the morning, I blew air out of my mouth and it looked frozen. All the flowers die in this season. Bears sleep until it is over.

8. Hand out a blank sheet of paper to each student. Tell them that they will have five minutes for writing. If they finish early, have them begin illustrating their paragraphs with drawings. After five minutes, have the students stop writing and double-check that their names are on their papers.

> *These short samples are from fifth graders in Fremont, California. For older students, you might require longer paragraphs that include even more subtle clues to the season. For example, part of a "spring" story could mention coming home from school blinking in the sunshine, putting away a dripping umbrella, having to vacuum the rug again because the dog is shedding like crazy, and then finding out the cat had kittens and there's asparagus for dinner.*

Get Out Your CD-ROM!

Stories of Seasons Around the World

Seasons around the world have inspired great literature and art. Enjoy stories about the seasons included on the CD-ROM or from your school's library/resource room.

Some of the greatest exploration adventures have been to areas of the world with extremes of seasons, such as the desert and the Arctic and Antarctic. The change of seasons is appreciated and respected by outdoor adventurers throughout the world. One group, sailing in January, 1915 on the ship *Endurance* to the Antarctic continent were particularly aware of what the changes in seasons were bringing. They were within one day of reaching Antactica when the heavy pack ice trapped their ship and then carried them north. The story of the survival of the Shackleton expedition to the Antarctic is one of the great adventure and leadership stories of our century.

On the CD-ROM is an excerpt from a book about the expedition and a link to a web site documenting the expedition using diary entries of Sir Ernest Shackleton, the expedition leader. Amazingly, many expedition photographs survived to document the extremes of the winter season in Antarctica. The expedition was rescued after a heroic 800-mile trip by Shackleton and a few crew members in a small boat through some of the most powerful gales on Earth.

To find out more, go to the CD Home screen and click on the item under Activity 1: *Stories of Seasons Around the World.*

Playing "Name the Season"

1. Remind students of Game Rules (c) and (d) and explain that they will have exactly five minutes to go around and read as many of the paragraphs as they can. Tell them that to get points in the game, they must write down on page 3 in their Seasons Lab Books by the name of the paragraph's author the correct season that the paragraph relates to. Say, "Ready, Set, Go." After five minutes say "Stop," and have them return to their seats.

If having everyone move around the classroom is difficult to manage, you can keep the class seated, and have volunteers read their paragraphs aloud while everyone else listens and writes down guesses. This does not have the time-element excitement of the "students-mobile" strategy, but will suffice if class management is an issue.

2. Have each student in turn state what season they had in mind so that the rest of the class can check their guesses. If time and student interest allow, have some or all of the students read their paragraphs aloud before they mention the season. Ask students not to change what they wrote as guesses in their Lab books, but only put an "X" by each wrong guess.

animals "wake up". flowers bloom, trees bud. baby animals are born. birds can migrate back. lots of rain. softball season starts! dandelions are everywhere!!! lots of mud.

all my friends are on vacation, my parents are at work, and my brother found a job. I locked my sister outside and I'm throwing water balloons at her from the top window. I snuck out the back door to get ice-cream, great, now she locked me out and is throwing the water balloons at me!

3. When all have shared, ask for some of the students' favorite seasonal clues used in the paragraphs, and add them to the chart on the chalkboard.

4. Have students count up the number of correct guesses they made.

Optional: Determine who won and give a prize to the winner. Have the student make illustrations of either their own paragraphs or those of other students.

Last night we went to a football game. Those cheerleaders must've been really cold. By the time the game was over, it was dark. It's starting to get darker earlier now. Pretty soon we'll even have to switch our clocks back! And those Halloween decorations in the stores are even better than last year's.

Get Out Your CD-ROM!

Trading Stories about the Seasons

At this web site you can study seasonal changes around the world! Students around the globe will study the changing seasons for four consecutive weeks through their own observations.
Each week, students:
    -Observe the new signs of seasonal change outside.
    -Discuss what they have seen.
    -Draw pictures and write stories for WWW publication

Students can publish their observations in a weekly WWW eZine. Students analyze the season's progress in their hemisphere and compare seasonal change in the hemisphere other than their own.

Just go to the CD Home screen and click on the item under Activity 1: *Trading Stories about the Seasons.*

Activity 2: Sun-Earth Survey

Part A

The short activity at the beginning of this session reinforces the students' understanding of the Earth's shape, its motion relative to the Sun, and what causes day and night. However, your students may need more experience with these concepts. If you have time, we strongly recommend that you precede the Seasons unit with the GEMS guide, Earth, Moon, and Stars, especially the first two class sessions.

Overview

Before they can understand what causes seasons, students need to know that the Earth is spherical, spins daily on its axis (rotates), and orbits the Sun (revolves). They also need to know what causes day and night. This class session starts with a brief activity to review these important, prerequisite concepts.

Students then answer questions on a short, written survey that focuses them on the following additional Sun-Earth concepts: the exact shape of the Earth's orbit and the distance between the Earth and the Sun. The survey also has a multiple choice question about the causes of seasons. For homework, students use the same survey questions on friends and family members. In the next session, the class will pool its data and discuss people's ideas about the seasons. (The survey approach is inspired in part by the Annenberg CPB project web pages at http://www.learner.org/teacherslab/).

Later in the unit, the answers to these survey questions will be revealed, as your students shed their own misconceptions, and surpass the Harvard grads in their understanding of what causes seasons!

What You Need—Part A

For the class:
- ❐ a light bulb, any size or wattage
- ❐ a lamp with no shade
- ❐ an extension cord
- ❐ 1 Earth globe

For each group of four to six students:
a piece of scratch paper and pencil

For each student:
- ❐ 1 "Seasons Survey" (p. 4 of Seasons Lab Book)
- ❐ 2 extra copies of the survey
- ❐ 1 pencil
- ❐ 1 pen
- ❐ (*Optional*) graph paper

Getting Ready

Plug in the lamp and set it on a table or chair in a part of the room where all the students can gather in a circle around it. If necessary, tape the cord to the floor to prevent students from tripping over it. It isn't necessary to darken the room. Have the Earth globe handy where you will introduce the activity.

Reviewing Some Key Sun-Earth Concepts

The Earth's Shape and Its Revolution Around the Sun

1. Ask, "Why is the Sun important?" [It provides warmth, light, energy, drives photosynthesis—without the Sun, there could not be life as we know it.] Tell the class that many ancient peoples worshipped or in some other way paid tribute to the Sun. Ask, "Why do you think they did that?"

2. While students are still seated at their desks, hold up a globe and ask, "If the Earth is shaped like a ball, why does it often look flat or hilly to us?" [We are very small compared to the size of the Earth, and the part we can see is only a very small part.]

3. Point to Australia on the globe, and ask why people living there don't "fall off." [Gravity pulls us all toward the center of the Earth, so everyone around the globe feels that the Earth is "down" and the sky is "up."]

4. Turn on the light bulb and turn off the room lights. Ask how the Earth moves in relation to the Sun. [The Earth revolves around the Sun in an orbit. It also spins or rotates on its axis.] Using the globe and light bulb, demonstrate these two motions. Ask how long one revolution around the Sun takes [one year], and how long Earth takes to spin once on its axis [24 hours]. How many 24 hour days in a year? [365]

5. Say that the light bulb and globe are a model to help us understand the motions of the Earth, but, of course, this model is not to scale. The Sun, represented by the by the lightbulb, is much bigger and hotter than the Earth, and much farther away than our model shows.

Night and Day on "Mount Nose"

1. Gather the students in a circle around the light bulb. Tell the class they will now use the light bulb model to explain what causes night and day. Instead of a globe, each of their heads will represent the Earth in the model.

2. Ask students to imagine their nose is a mountain and that a person lives on the tip of "Mount Nose." With the students facing the light bulb, ask, "For the person standing on your Mount Nose, where in the sky is the Sun?" [high in the sky, over the person's head] Ask, "What time of day do you think it is for the person on Mount Nose?" [noon]

3. Ask students to turn to their left, and stop when their right ears are facing the Sun. Ask, "For the person on Mt. Nose, where in the sky does the Sun seem to be? [near the horizon, low in the sky] Ask, "What time of day is it for the person?" [sunset]

> *This "Mount Nose" activity is taken from the* Earth, Moon, and Stars *GEMS guide.*

4. Have students continue to turn, stopping when their backs are to the light bulb. Ask, "What time is it for the person on Mt. Nose?" [around midnight] "On what part of your head is it daytime?" [the back of your head because it is now facing the Sun]

5. Have the students make another quarter turn, so that their left ears face the Sun. "Where is the Sun in the sky now? [low in the sky, just 'coming up'] What time is it" [sunrise] Have the class turn back to face the light.

6. Have the students rotate through one more day, observing as the Sun seems to set and rise. Have everyone return to their seats.

The Sun-Earth Survey

1. Say that most people understand that the Earth revolves around the Sun once a year, and how the spinning of the Earth causes day and night. **However, most people, including adults, don't understand and cannot explain why seasons happen.**

2. Tell the class that a group of Harvard graduates were asked what caused the seasons. They thought they knew, and explained with great confidence, but most of them had mistaken ideas. Tell the class that in a week or so, you hope they will know more than Harvard graduates (at least about seasons)!

3. Tell the class that before studying why seasons occur, they will first answer a few questions on a survey themselves. Emphasize that this is not for a grade. If they don't yet understand what causes the seasons, they are just like most people. Later as they learn more about the seasons, they will look back at these questions.

4. Tell the students to write their answers in ink. Have them open their Seasons Lab Books to the survey on page 4 and begin. Tell them that if they don't know an answer, a careful guess is okay, but they should be ready to explain why they picked the answers they did. When they've circled all their answers, they should discuss their thinking with a partner. Have them begin.

Important Note: The correct responses to the survey can be found in the "Behind the Scenes" background for teachers section, page 89, along with some information that can help you interpret what various student responses may indicate about their thinking. Because many students may have guessed an answer (sometimes correctly), a discussion of the rationale behind their responses is necessary and valuable in bringing out their thinking.

While students will be curious about the answers considered to be most correct by scientists, **refrain from revealing the correct responses now.** Instead, tell them they will find out the answers to these and other important, related questions as they do the upcoming activities in *The Real Reasons for Seasons* unit.

Surveying Family and Friends

1. Regain the attention of the whole class, and hold a discussion. For each of the survey questions, ask a volunteer to tell what they answered and why. Ask if other students agree, or have alternate answers or different thoughts. As students share their views, ask probing questions like, "Would you explain your reasoning?"

2. Explain that you aren't going to tell them the answers that scientists would consider correct now, because you want them to continue to think about the questions. Explain that the upcoming activities in the *Seasons* unit will not only help them discover the correct answers for themselves, but will also help them understand why!

3. Tell the students they will each get two copies of the survey to take home and use with two friends or family members. They should tell their survey subjects that they are about to begin a unit on what causes seasons, and are gathering data about what most people think. They can tell people their responses will be anonymous, and that they shouldn't feel embarrassed if they aren't sure of the answers, because that's very common.

4. Pass out two blank surveys per student. Ask them to bring in the completed surveys by the next class session.

Get Out Your CD-ROM!

Student Misconceptions and Conceptual Development

The importance of student misconceptions about the seasons cannot be overstressed. Student misconceptions in this area have fueled the field of research on student misconceptions in math and science. Several international research conferences have been held on misconceptions. Summaries of papers presented at these conferences are on the web through the Meaningful Learning Research Group site at http://www2.ucsc.edu/mlrg/mlrghome.html

The Private Universe Project has explored misconceptions about the seasons. The film "A Private Universe" was created and produced by Matthew H. Schneps and Philip M. Sadler, Harvard-Smithsonian Center for Astrophysics.

On the CD-ROM are links to Web addresses on:
- **A Private Universe Project**—Annenberg CPB Teacher's Lab web page which inspired our survey
- Misconception research
- An excellent paper on the "Cognitive Aspects of Learning and Teaching Science" by Jose P. Mestre of the Department of Physics & Astronomy at the University of Massachusetts – Amherst. This paper addresses the seasons and misconceptions in teaching science.

To get to the above web pages, just go to the CD Home screen and click on the item under Activity 2: *Student Misconceptions and Conceptual Development.*

Sun-Earth Survey

1. Which of the four drawings do you think best shows the shape of Earth's orbit around the Sun? (The view is top down.) Circle the correct letter.

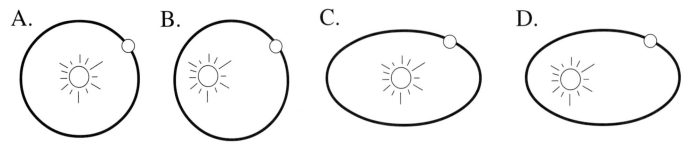

A.　　　　B.　　　　C.　　　　D.

2. Which is the best drawing to show the sizes and distances between the Earth and the Sun? Circle the letter of the best drawing.

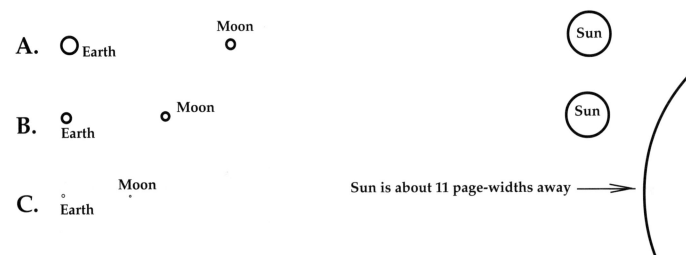

A.　O Earth　　　　Moon ○

B.　o Earth　　　　o Moon

C.　Earth　　Moon

Sun is about 11 page-widths away ⟶

3. Why do you think it is hotter in the United States in June than in December?
   Circle all that are correct.

   A. Because the Sun itself gives off more heat and light energy in June and less in December.

   B. Because the Earth is closer to the Sun in June, and farther away from the Sun in December.

   C. Because the United States is closer to the Sun in June and farther from the Sun in December.

   D. Because the United States is facing more toward the Sun in June and away from the Sun in December.

   E. Because the Sun gets higher in the sky in June, so its rays are more concentrated on the ground.

   F. Because the Moon blocks out the Sun more in December.

   G. Because in the United States, there are more hours of daylight in June than in December.

 　　　　LHS GEMS: *The Real Reasons for Seasons*

Part B: The Results of the Survey

Overview

In this part of the activity, students pool the data from the Sun-Earth surveys. They work in groups to tally the results, then determine the class totals. Each student prepares a graph to represent the results of the survey.

What You Need
For the class:
❐   *(Optional)* 3 calculators

For each student:
❐   Seasons Lab Book with their own completed survey
❐   the completed surveys of their friends and family
❐   pencil
❐   graph paper
❐   colored markers

For each group of 4–6 students:
❐   a piece of scratch paper

Getting Ready
Plan to group the students in groups of from four to six students.

Pooling the Data from Sun-Earth Surveys

1. Have students take out their own completed surveys in their lab books, as well as the two surveys completed by friends and family.

2. The goal of this activity is to try to come to some conclusions about what everyone surveyed thinks about seasons. Say they'll first add up their data from the surveys in small groups. To do this, they will first choose a recorder for their small group. Starting with question #1, each student will tell the recorder how many responses they got for answers A, B, C, and D. The recorder will tally them on a piece of scratch paper. They will tally the totals for all questions on the survey in this way.

> If each student has three completed surveys, a group of four students will have 12 answers total for question #1. (Note that there may be more than 12 answers for #3, since respondents can make more than one choice for that question.)

3. When everyone has finished their small group tallies, regain the attention of the whole class, and ask each recorder to give you their group's totals. Quickly record these on the overhead or chalkboard. Ask volunteers to calculate the grand totals of responses from the whole class. Record these on the chalkboard for each question.

4. Ask students what they can conclude from the data. Accept all answers, encouraging them to make generalizations. [For example: There was an big split in opinion on question #1, especially between answers A and C.] Ask, "Were any of the results surprising to you? Why?"

5. Say that each student will make a graph to represent the totals for each survey question (three graphs per student). Allow students to choose how to represent the data—bar, pie, or other types of graphs are fine.

6. Ask for suggestions from students about what information should be included on the graph, how to fit all the data onto the paper, labels needed, and a title. You may want to make a sample graph together on the chalkboard for one of the questions. Depending on time and student experience with graphing, assign some or all of the graphs as homework.

7. When all the graphs are complete, ask students to display samples of a variety of graphs for each of the survey questions. Ask the class for some observations. Did graphing the data make it easier to see the results of the survey? Were there any new surprises?

8. End the class by telling the students that in the next few days they will find out if the majority opinions on the survey agree or disagree with the answers that most scientists would give.

Get Out Your CD-ROM!

Stanford Solar Center and Solar Folklore

The Stanford Solar Center is a great web site for investigations about the Sun, featuring NASA's SOHO satellite mission. The web site has educational activities and a great set of links. It even has a whole area on solar folklore from a wide variety of cultures.

Just go to the CD Home screen and click on the item under Activity 2:
Stanford Solar Center and Solar Folklore

Activity 3: Trip to the Sun

Overview

In this activity, the class takes a "trip" to the Sun together by viewing a series of 14 images. They leave San Francisco at sunrise, and travel directly towards the Sun in a straight line (with the Sun on the horizon). At each step or "observation point," students monitor their distance traveled and their altitude above Earth. In the first part of the journey, as they speed along in a straight line over the United States, their altitude above the Earth increases, due to the spherical shape of the Earth. A main goal of the activity is for students to reinforce their conception of the Earth's spherical shape, which is key to understanding the cause of the seasons.

The scale of the Earth-Sun system is also key to understanding seasons. As students continue their journey to the Sun, they get a sense of the great distance they travel. They then create a scale model to reinforce the idea that the distance to the Sun is enormous compared with the size of the Earth. Finally, they reflect on Question 3 of the Sun-Earth Survey and decide if they would now change their response.

The path of this imaginary trip toward the Sun is very different from flying east in an airplane. If we fly from San Francisco to New York in an airplane, we stay relatively close to the Earth, and our flight path curves along with the Earth.

What You Need

For the class:
❐ 1 overhead projector or CD-ROM disk used with the whole class at once (see note at right, "Get Out your CD-ROM)
❐ 7 pages of overhead transparencies for "Trip to the Sun" (masters on pages 31–43)
OR
❐ CD-ROM disk
❐ 1 scale model (a car or any toy made to scale is fine)
❐ 1 Model Sun (28 cm diameter) drawn on manila file folder; to make this the first time, you need:
___ 1 manila file folder
___ 1 marking pen, wide tipped
___ 1 strip of card stock, about 1 cm x 16 cm
___ 1 pushpin
___ 1 small piece of corrugated cardboard, at least 5 cm square

❐ one Earth globe or large ball * **(see note below)**
❐ 1 ruler, any type

For each student:
❐ 1 "Trip to the Sun" worksheets (pp. 5–8 of Seasons Lab Book)
❐ 1 pencil
❐ *(Optional)* 1 calculator

* Inflatable globes don't work well for the demonstration at the end of this activity. You will need a hard-surfaced Earth globe. A soccer ball, basketball, or other rigid, large ball will also work.

Get Out Your CD-ROM!

Trip to the Sun Slide Show
For images to use in the Trip to the Sun, you have the option of using either the CD-ROM slide show or a series of overhead transparencies. The CD-ROM option is far superior, since the images are in color with fairly high resolution. If you choose to use the CD-ROM version, be sure that you have a way for all students to see the images at one time, either on a single large screen visible to all, or on multiple computers in a computer lab. To call up the slide show, just go to the CD Home screen and click on the item under Activity 3:
Trip to the Sun Slide Show

Getting Ready

1. Decide on whether you will use overhead transparencies or the CD-ROM. If using the CD-ROM, check to be sure the images can be seen by the whole class. A projection system is the best option, either a video computer projector or an overhead projector LCD display. If this is not possible in your circumstances, the next best option would be to display the images on a single large monitor (21 inches or more) and have the class gather around.

2. Draw a circle 28 cm in diameter. Make two marks separated by 14 cm on a strip of cardstock. Insert a pushpin through the one of the marks and enlarge it so that a pencil tip will fit through. Then stick the pushpin through the other mark. Use the cardstock strip as a compass to draw the circle on a piece of paper. Then go over the circle with a felt-tipped pen for better visibility. (If you make one of the holes in the cardstock large enough, you can use the felt-tipped pen instead of a pencil to draw the original circle.)

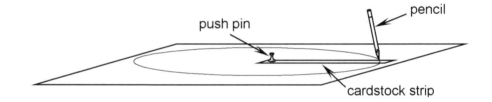

push pin   pencil

cardstock strip

3. Decide if it will be possible to take the class outside for a short scale model activity at the end of the session. If time, weather, or other considerations make that impossible, spend a few minutes before class finding a spot that is about 30 meters away from the classroom. Do this by pacing off 30 long strides in a straight line. It's helpful if the spot is easy to describe to students, like an object outside that is visible from the classroom window or something that is down the hall from the classroom.

Get Out Your CD-ROM!

Views of Earth

A trip to the Sun from San Francisco would cross the United States and give a great view of the land. NASA astronauts and satellites in orbit (typically about 400 miles above the Earth for some common photographic satellites) have taken spectacular photos. These satellite pictures are taken through a variety of filters and are not meant to look like what the eye would see from orbit. The colors are often manipulated to bring out the greatest contrast to see different agricultural and mineralogical features. To get to the images taken by astronauts and satellite, just go to the CD Home screen and click on the item under Activity 3: *Views of Earth.*

Distance Traveled: 0.0 km   **Altitude: 0.3 km**

View Towards Sun:

View Towards Earth's Center:

San Francisco, California

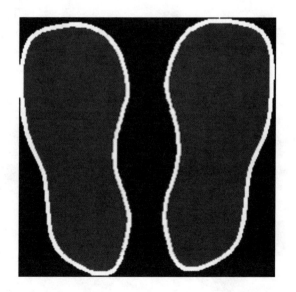

Distance Traveled: 100 km   Altitude:1 km

**View Towards
Sun:**

**View Towards
Earth's Center:**   **Sacramento Area, California**

View Towards Sun:

View Towards Earth's Center: Walker Lake, Nevada

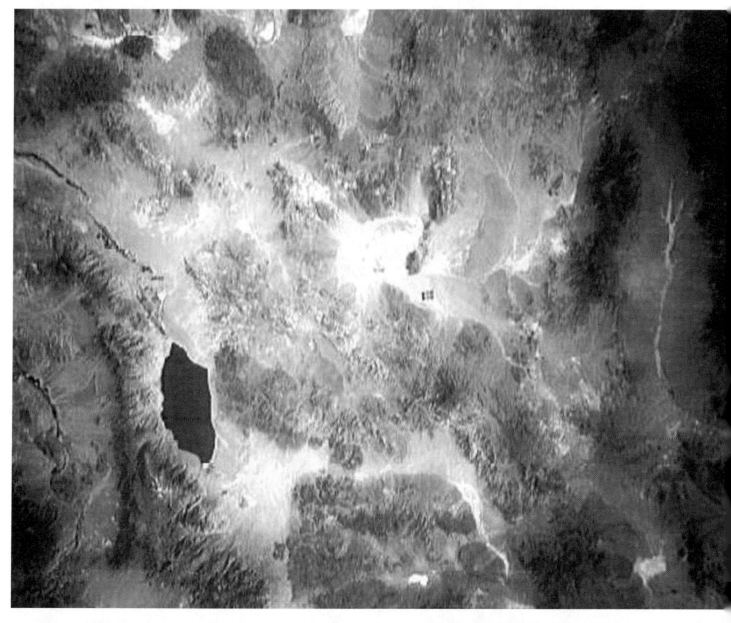

4 Distance Traveled: 1950 km   Altitude: 290 km

View Towards Sun:

View Towards Earth's Center: Denver, Colorado

5 Distance Traveled: 4000 km   Altitude: 1200 km

**View Towards
Sun:**

**View Towards
Earth's Center:**   **St. Louis —Mississippi River**

**View Towards
Sun:**

**View Towards
Earth's Center:**   **Massachusetts, Cape Cod**

7 Distance Traveled: 20,000 km   Altitude: 14,000 km

View Towards Sun:

View Towards Earth: Atlantic Ocean, Mir Space Station

View
Towards
Sun:

View
Towards
Earth:

9   Distance Traveled: 500,000 km   Altitude: 494,000 km

View Towards Sun:

**View
Towards
Earth:**

10 Distance Traveled: 120 million km Altitude: 120 million km

View Towards Sun: (sunspots visible)

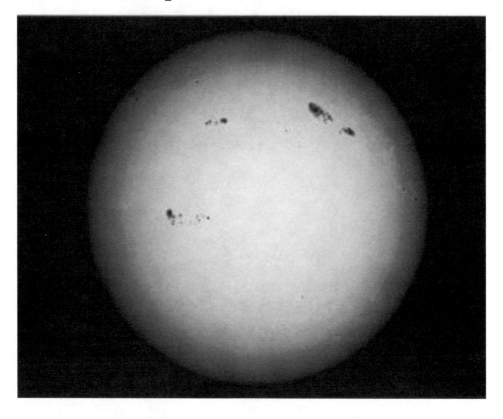

View Towards Earth:

View Towards Sun:
(sunspots, flares, prominences, and granulation visible)

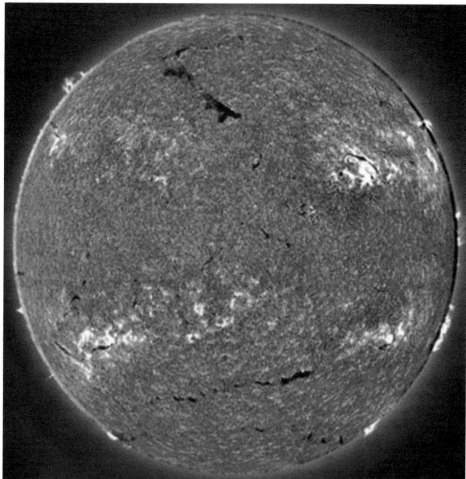

View Towards Earth:

**View
Towards
Sun:**

**(close-up of a
flare)**

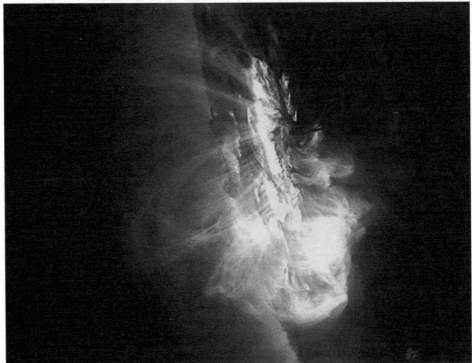

**View
Towards
Earth:**

A Trip to the Sun

1. Explain to the students that they are going to take a short "trip to the Sun," starting in San Francisco, California at sunrise and traveling in a straight line towards the Sun. Ask, "Which direction is the Sun at sunrise: north, south, east, or west?" [East.]

2. Explain to the class that they will be in an imaginary spaceship, traveling from San Francisco to the Sun. They will make 12 observations along the trip. At each observation point, or step in the journey, two views are provided: one towards the Sun and one towards the center of the Earth. Also at each observation point, we will be able to note the distance traveled along our flight path as well as our distance above the ground (also known as our *altitude*). Spend a little time verifying that your students understand what altitude means. Have them imagine they are in a helicopter that takes off straight up and climbs at a speed of one kilometer per hour. What would the helicopter's altitude be after 1/2 hour?

3. Explain that our spaceship will *not* take off vertically—we will start out moving mostly horizontally, straight towards the Sun which is just rising over the hills east of San Francisco. Have students turn to the "Trip to the Sun" section in their Seasons Lab Books (pages 5–8). Display the first image on the CD or turn on the overhead projector and show the top half of the first transparency. Point out the view towards the Sun and note the crescent moon positioned near the Sun. The view downwards in the first image just shows our feet at ground level (altitude 0.3 km).

4. Ask the students to record the "Distance Traveled" and the "Altitude" in the "Step 1" row in the Lab Book. If necessary, review the definition of a kilometer as compared with a mile: 1 km = 0.62 mile and 1 mile = 1.6 km. (Roughly, a mile is "half again bigger" than a kilometer, or a kilometer is about 5/8 of a mile.) We've chosen to use kilometers because that is the international standard, and it is best to use it if we want to communicate with anyone anywhere in the world, especially in science. Remind the students that we are going to travel directly towards the Sun (east) in a straight line.

5. Start the journey, showing the images and information at each of the observation points. Point out the small crescent shape near the Sun and ask, "What might that be?" [The Moon.] For each observation point, ask:

- Has the view towards the Sun changed?

- What do we see in our view towards the center of the Earth?

- You might ask if students have any friends or relatives in the places they see in the first six observation points.

Some Optional Math/Physics Opportunities: On their journey to the Sun, students could compute their speed at each observation point, dividing distance traveled (since the previous observation) by time elapsed. If you arbitrarily choose a one hour time between observations, speed then comes out in km/hr. Or, at the end of the journey, students could compute the average speed for each section of the trip by subtracting the distance traveled at each step from the distance traveled in the previous step and dividing that by time elapsed, e.g. one minute (1/60 of an hour) for each step. You could make a table showing this. Make sure students realize that most of these speeds are not possible for human travel. Here's an example:

Average Speed	=	Distance Traveled	÷	Time Elapsed
V	=	D	÷	T

Step	Distance (thousands) of km	Speed (thousands of) km/hr
1	0	0
2	0.10	6
3	0.45	21
4	1.95	90
5	4.0	123
6	7.0	180
7	20	780
8	300	16,800
9	500	12,000
10	120,000	7,200,000
11	130,000	600,000
12	140,000	600,000

6. At each point, have students record the "Distance Traveled," the "Altitude," and in the proper row in the Lab Book. To give students a sense of their altitude in the first few steps, tell them:

- the height of Mount Everest is just over 29,000 feet or about 8.8 km (5 1/2 miles)

- At step 3 over Nevada, mention that our altitude of 15 km is already much higher than the altitude at which most passenger jets fly (about 10 km).

- At step 4, say that we are almost as high as the orbit of the space shuttle (320 km).

- At step 7, we are really "leaving Earth." Notice the curvature of Earth as we reach a high enough altitude.

7. At step 8, as we look back at Earth, ask "What is the diameter of Earth?" [It's about 12,500 km or 8,000 miles] If necessary, review what the term diameter means—distance across a circle through the center of the circle).

8. There is an interesting change-over that happens between steps 8 and 9 as we pass the Moon. There is a reversal in the phase of the Moon. Why is it a crescent in step 8, but nearly full in step 9? This is a view of the full moon that we would not normally see from Earth—it is the "far side" of the Moon. (*The moon is about 400,000 km from Earth.*)

9. In image 9, the Moon appears to be bigger than Earth. Is it really? [No.] Why does it look bigger here? [It's closer to us.]

10. From image 10 onwards, we execute a plunge into the Sun. In image 10 we can see sunspots; in image 11, granulation in the Sun's surface; and in image 12, solar flares. The view back towards Earth shows only a planet Earth dot.

11. As you finish the trip, mention that it's a good thing this has been an imaginary trip. Ask what would happen if we flew too close to the Sun. [We'd plunge into the Sun and die.]

Reflecting on the Trip to the Sun

1. Ask, "Did our altitude increase in the first several steps? [Yes. Not much in step 2, but after that, it increased fast.]

2. Ask a student to list the altitudes above the Earth for the first six steps of the journey, while you record them on the chalkboard:

0.3 km in San Francisco
1 km over Sacramento
15 km over Nevada
290 km over Denver, Colorado
1200 km over St. Louis, Missouri
3155 km over New York City.

3. Choose a spot in the room to represent the Sun. Remind the students that we didn't take off straight up from San Francisco. Hold up a globe and point to San Francisco. Hold the globe with San Francisco facing directly towards the Sun. Ask what time it is in San Francisco. [noon, because the Sun is overhead] Use a ruler to show the kind of vertical take-off that we *didn't* do.

4. Challenge the class to help you use the ruler and globe to show how we *did* take off from San Francisco at sunrise, and how we traveled in a straight line east towards the rising Sun:

a. Spin the globe until San Francisco is facing directly away from the "Sun" and ask what time it is there now. [midnight]

b. Spin the globe a quarter turn more, so that San Francisco is getting its first glimpse of the Sun in the east [sunrise] and stop.

c. Ask a student volunteer to position the ruler and the globe so that the ruler represents the path of the first six steps or more of the "Trip to the Sun." [One end of the ruler should touch San Francisco, and the other end should point to the "Sun." Because the globe is curved, most of the ruler will not be touching the ground, and its distance from the ground will increase as it goes east over the United States.]

d. Ask, "If we were traveling in a straight line east toward the Sun, why did our altitude above the ground increase?" [Our path was a straight line, **but the Earth's surface is curved— Earth is a ball.** As we flew in a straight line toward the Sun, the Earth's surface curved away from us.]

5. Give students a few minutes to write in their lab books why we gained altitude in the first six steps of the trip to the Sun. Have them make drawings to help illustrate their explanations. As they are doing this, take the globe and ruler around the room so all students can see up close that the ruler is farther from the ground over New York than Denver.

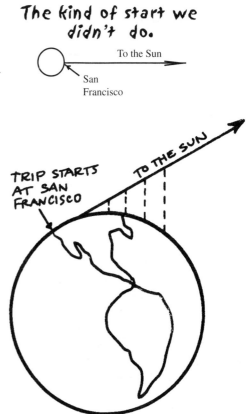

The kind of start we didn't do.

To the Sun

San Francisco

TRIP STARTS AT SAN FRANCISCO

TO THE SUN

Spin the globe in a counterclockwise direction, when seen from above the North Pole. It's fine to hold the globe with the North Pole straight up (not tilted) for this demonstration.

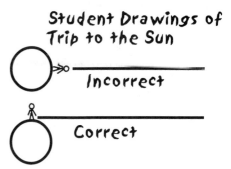

Student Drawings of Trip to the Sun

Incorrect

Correct

Get Out Your CD-ROM!

Curvature of the Earth

The curvature of the Earth limits the distance one can see to the horizon. On the CD-ROM is information on how far one can see from different height, with a formula to calculate the distance to the horizon. This is a good math exercise for students. Just go to the CD Home screen and click on the item under Activity 3: *Curvature of the Earth*

If time allows, you might want to give your students the actual diameters and distances and ask them to compute the scale model's diameters and distances. Tell them that if Earth is only 0.25 cm, the scale of that model is 1 cm = 50,000 km. Have them divide the values below by 50,000: [Moon optional]

	Diameter [in km]	Distance from Earth
Earth	12,750	0
Moon	3,480	384,400
Sun	1,390,000	149,600,000

If you are not able to take the class outside, tell them the location of the spot 30 meters away that you previously paced off.

A Sun-Earth Scale Model

1. Tell the students that you would like for them to get a true sense of the distance from the Earth to the Sun by making a quick scale model of the Sun-Earth system. Say that scientists often use scale models to help them understand things they have difficulty observing directly. Hold up the scale model car, and explain that someone measured a real car, and made everything smaller by the same amount. We can look at a scale model, and get a good idea of what the real thing looks like. Mention that the Earth globe is a scale model too.

2. If we made a scale model where 50,000 km = 1 cm, the Earth would be much smaller than the classroom globe: 0.25 cm in diameter, or about the size of a pinhead. Make a dot of about 0.25 cm on the chalkboard to represent Earth, and ask, "At this scale, how big do you think the Sun would be?" After accepting a few guesses, hold up the 28 cm diameter circle you cut out earlier. (Be sure students understand that the Sun is a ball, like Earth.)

3. Ask "At the same scale (50,000 km = 1 cm), how far away from Earth do you think the Sun is?

4. Ask students for some guesses of how far away would the Sun have to be. Tell the students that at this scale, the Sun would be about *30 meters* from the Earth.

5. Explain that a meter in very rough terms is about one "pace," about the distance of one large step as one is walking. Ask, "Would the scale distance to the Sun, 30 paces, fit in the classroom?" [no]

6. If time and other conditions permit, invite the students to go outside onto the playground to pace off the distance to the Sun in this scale model. Tape the paper sun to a fence or wall. Together, walk 30 paces from the paper sun. Have students notice that when they stand 30 meters from the paper sun, it looks about the same size as the real Sun in the sky.

7. Remind the class of the size of the Earth at this scale: about the size of the head of a pin. Say that the Moon would be a speck one quarter the size of the Earth. It would be about eight centimeters away from the Earth. Have them try to imagine how much bigger the scale of the real Sun-Earth system is.

8. Refer back to question #2 on the Sun-Earth Survey. Which drawing most accurately represents the Sun-Earth distance? [C]

9. Refer to question #3 on the Sun-Earth survey. Explain that some people may have picked answer C (the United States is closer in June) but not B (Earth is closer). How could that be? (If some students have responded in this way, encourage them to explain their reasoning.) If their response includes a reference to the Earth's tilt, for example [The United States is tilted toward the Sun in June and away from the Sun in December] then ask, "Does a tilt of the Earth really make the United States closer enough in summer to make a big difference in temperature?" Have students compare the diameter of Earth with the distance to the Sun and consider this last question as they continue with the activities in the unit.

Get Out Your CD-ROM!

A Real Trip to the Sun. People have been dreaming about a trip to the Sun for hundreds or even thousands of years. However, once it was learned that the Sun is an incredibly hot ball of gas, the difficulties of such a trip became apparent. Although astronomers have relied on telescopes to study the Sun, there are some things about the Sun that are best studied by going there. NASA has begun design work on the Solar Probe Mission, a spacecraft designed to actually go on a journey to the Sun. Read more about the Solar Probe and how it will be designed in an illustrated article called Journey to the Sun on the CD-ROM. NASA also has a website on the Solar Probe Mission that will provide updates to the launch date and progress of the mission. A link to the web site is included on the CD-ROM.

Sun Facts Table: On the CD-ROM is a table of Sun facts, including the size, density, distance, and temperature of the Sun.

What is the Sun Really Like? A slide show on the Sun is available on the CD-ROM. It has many high-quality color images of the Sun taken by x-ray and ultraviolet telescopes. The first half of the show may be of the greatest interest as the second half is more technical.

Movies of the Sun in Action: Telescopes in space have been able to capture images of the Sun in action. View some of these movies to see what can be seen using space instruments. They are listed in the next column.

Solar Images from NASA's SoHO-LASCO satellite: This film shows the Sun ejecting a cloud of plasma, a comet being destroyed, and the Milky Way in the background

X-Rays and White Light Images of the Sun: A comparison of how the Sun looks in X-ray and visible light showing how sunspots and X-ray regions are related on a rotating Sun.

Solar Eclipse from Space: The GOES7 weather satellite shot this sequence that shows the shadow of the solar eclipse tracking across the face of Earth. Go through the frames of the movie slowly to watch the path of the eclipse.

Space Station Tour 2: On the way to the Sun, our journey might come within sight of the International Space Station. This animation shows what such a close approach might look like.

SoHO-LASCO Mass Ejection from the Sun: Solar material was ejected from the Sun on April 7, 1997 and seen by this satellite.

Rotating Solar Disk viewed by the light from ionized iron atoms.

The Solar Wind: animation of solar wind emerging from granulation cells on solar surface.

Magnetosphere Fly-Through Animation, by DC Spensley: This animation shows a trip from the Sun to the Earth, with a fly-through of the major parts of the Earth's environment.

To see these resources, just go to the CD Home screen
and click on the item under
Activity 3: *What is the Sun Really Like?*

Get Out Your CD-ROM!

Scale Models of the Earth-Moon System and the Solar System

Scale Models of the Earth-Moon System and the Solar System are important tools for understanding the vast distances in astronomy. Many people picture the Earth, Moon, and Sun as very close together—they are not. The Moon is located about a distance of about 30 times the diameter of the Earth away from the Earth. The Sun is located nearly 400 times the distance of the Earth to the Moon. Several web sites are referenced on the CD-ROM which allow one to construct scale models.

The Earth-Moon System to Scale web site allows one to construct a scale model of the Earth-Moon System.

The Exploratorium's "Build a Solar System" Page
allows you to build a solar system model (including the Moon and the satellites of the planets) at any scale:

To get to either of these websites, just go to the CD Home screen and click on the item under Activity 3:
Scale Models, Earth-Moon, and Solar System

Activity 4: What Shape is Earth's Orbit?

Overview

In this session, students discover that the true shape of the Earth's orbit around the Sun is very nearly a perfect circle. This begins to dispel a common misconception that seasons are caused by variation in the distance from the Sun to the Earth. Students look back at the results of the class survey on this question, and reflect on why so many people think the seasons have to do with the Earth's distance from the Sun.

What You Need

For every pair of students:
- ❒ a 25 cm piece string or twine—not stretchy
- ❒ 1 pencil
- ❒ 3 sheets of blank paper (or 2 sheets and page 9 of Seasons Lab Books)
- ❒ 2 push pins or thumb tacks
- ❒ a stack of newspaper, at least the thickness of the pins or tacks students will use

For the class:
- ❒ 1 40 cm piece string or twine— not stretchy
- ❒ a bulletin board or chart paper pad
- ❒ one piece of paper at least 14 x 14 inches
- ❒ two push pins or thumbtacks
- ❒ 1 overhead transparency of 3 ellipses and comet
- ❒ 1 blank overhead transparency
- ❒ 2 different colored transparency pens
- ❒ 1 hula hoop *or* large round embroidery hoop
- ❒ scratch paper to draw extra ellipses

Getting Ready

1. Make the 40 cm piece of string into a loop by tying the ends together so that the loop measures 17 cm when stretched flat. An easy way to do this is to stick two push pins in a thick piece of cardboard, 17 cm apart, and tie the string around the push pins. Test to make sure the knot won't slip. Once you have made a set of string loops, they may be used over and over again for many classes.

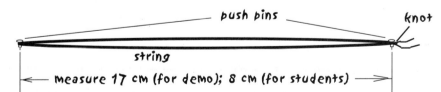

2. You'll need one smaller loop per pair of students. Cut one 25 cm piece of string per pair of students. Decide if you or a volunteer will tie the loops, or if you will have students tie them at the beginning of the activity. If students will tie them, you'll need to provide rulers for them to measure the loops.

3. Put a large piece of paper at least 14 x 14 inches on the bulletin board. It needs to be placed in an area where the class can see it during your demonstration. It also needs to be mounted where you can push two pins into the surface. If you don't have a bulletin board, you may need to put cardboard or another such surface onto the wall for this demonstration. Use the steps in #4 below to practice drawing an ellipse before class.

The Shape of the Earth's Orbit

1. Tell the class that in this session, they will learn about the shape of the Earth's orbit around the Sun. This knowledge will help them later as they zero in on what really causes the seasons. Draw on the board (or use transparency of) three orbit shapes and label them as shown below:

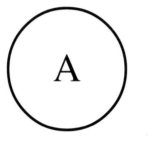

2. Poll the students, "Which drawing most correctly shows the shape of the Earth's orbit.around the Sun: A, B, or C?" [If they have heard that it is an ellipse or oval, it is likely they will choose B or C.]

3. Explain that an *ellipse* is an oval shape, but a very precise and symmetrical oval. Tell the class they will draw a couple of ellipses representing real orbits of Earth and Pluto, which both revolve around the Sun in the solar system. The goal is to find out the shape of each orbit, and how much Earth's orbit deviates from a perfect circle. Tell the students that you will demonstrate how to draw an ellipse by drawing the orbit of a comet.

4. Demonstrate how to draw an ellipse as follows:

    a. Make two pen marks 12 cm apart on the large paper on the bulletin board.

    b. Stick a push pin through each pen mark and into the bulletin board.

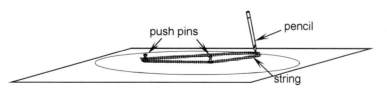

    c. Drape the string loop you made from a 40 cm piece of string over the push pins.

    d. Ask for a volunteer at this point to hold one of the push pins steady.

    e. Hold the other push pin steady and pull the string taut with the tip of a marking pen.

f. Draw the ellipse, keeping the string taut at all times. Emphasize while you are drawing the importance of keeping the string taut as you draw the ellipse as well as having two people work together to make sure the push pins stay firmly in place while making the ellipse.

5. Explain that each point where a push pin goes in is called a *focus* of the ellipse. Mention that the plural of focus is *foci* (FOE- sigh). Point out that the comet orbit that you drew is fairly "skinny, or elongated, not circular." Explain also that in the orbits of planets (as well as comets or asteroids) the Sun remains fixed at only one of the foci of the ellipse.

6. Explain that they will each draw the shapes of orbits of Earth and Pluto in their lab books. Emphasize that the drawings are not to scale—that Pluto's orbit is actually almost 40 times the diameter of Earth's orbit, but for now we only want to compare the *shapes* of the orbits. They will work with a partner, and take turns; one will help keep the push pins steady while the other is drawing. Each pair of students will get a string loop, two push pins, and a stack of newspaper. Demonstrate how to place the open page of a lab book on the pad of newspaper so that the pins won't damage the desk tops.

7. Say that Pluto and Earth have foci separations of 5 cm and 0.4 cm respectively, as noted on page 9 of their Lab Books. Distribute materials to each pair and have them begin. *Optional:* Ask those who finish quickly to draw additional orbits on scratch paper with foci separations of 2, 3, 4, or 6 centimeters.

8. Have one early finisher draw the Pluto and Earth orbits on a blank transparency using two colors of pen. Label the orbits "Pluto" and "Earth" using corresponding colors of pens. When everyone has finished, collect the string, newspaper and push pins.

Dispelling a Common Misconception About Earth's Orbit

1. Put the transparency with both the Earth's and Pluto's orbits on the overhead projector. Ask, "Is Earth's orbit really larger than Pluto's?" [No, it's actually *much* smaller.] Remind them that we are concentrating here only on the **shapes** of the orbits.

2. Ask, "Which orbit is more circular, Pluto's or Earth's?" [Earth's] Explain that, while it is true that Earth's orbit is slightly elliptical, it is very nearly a circular ellipse. Pluto has the least circular orbit of all the planets, and it still looks pretty circular. Comets have orbits that are more skinny ellipses than the orbits of planets.

> **Definition of an Ellipse**
> *In math, an ellipse is defined as a set of points that have the property that the sum of their respective distances from two points (the focus points) is constant. The "constant" in this definition is given physical meaning in our ellipse drawing activity by the fixed length of string used to connect the two foci. Note that if the two focus points are brought together onto one point, then this definition reduces to "a set of points whose distance to a particular point is constant"—the definition of a circle! In other words, a circle is a type of ellipse for which both foci are at the same point: the center of the circle.*

> *It is an interesting fact that because of the non-circularity of Pluto's orbit, it became the 8th planet from the Sun in the period from about February 8, 1979 to about March 11, 1999. In that time interval, Pluto's distance from the Sun was less than Neptune's.*

3. Have the class look back at the class results and their graphs from question #1 on the survey in their lab books:

Which of the four drawings do you think best shows the shape of Earth's orbit around the Sun?

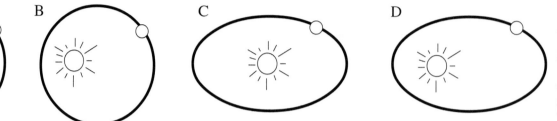

4. Ask, "Did many people choose either answer C or D?" "What is wrong with those answers? [We've just found that the Earth's orbit is very close to a circle.]

5. Ask students where the Sun should be in their drawings of Earth's and Pluto's orbits. [the center, because if the Sun is always at a focus of the ellipse and the foci are very close together and centered in the ellipses, then the Sun is very close to the center of the ellipse.] Reveal that, not only is the Earth's orbit almost circular, but the Sun is in the center of the orbit. So, when considering survey question #1's answers A and B, which is correct? [A]

The distance from the Earth to the Sun does not change much relative to the entire distance. But Earth is actually closest to the Sun on January 4!

6. Ask students why they think many people pick answers C or D. [Drawings of the solar system in books and on posters often make the orbits look like fairly skinny ellipses. This is because the orbits are drawn from the side, as though viewed at an angle.] Use a hula hoop or a large embroidery hoop to demonstrate how the shape *appears* to change depending on the angle at which you view it.

7. Tell the students that if you ask people, "What causes seasons?" most of them say something like, "The Earth is closer to the Sun in summer, farther from the Sun in winter." Perhaps this is why many people choose answers B, C, or D: The distance between Earth and Sun varies in these drawings.

8. Remind students of Question 3 of the Sun-Earth Survey: "Why do you think it is hotter in New York in June than in December?" Ask how many people the class surveyed picked answer B, *Because the Earth is closer to the Sun in June, and farther away from the Sun in December.* [Probably many] Emphasize that being closer to the Sun is not why we have summer. In fact, we are closest to the Sun on January 4, wintertime in the Northern Hemisphere.

Going Further (Images needed on next two pages)

Apparent Changes in the Sun's Size with Season

If people believe that the Sun is closer to Earth in the summer, then it should appear larger during the summer. Have your students measure how much the Sun's size appears to change using real photographs of the Sun at different seasons (masters on the following two pages). One teacher who presented this activity said that his students had a sense of being *real* astronomers because they were using *real* photographs of the Sun.

First have students guess how much change they might measure in the apparent size of the Sun during the year. (Worksheet master: bottom half of this page.) If 100% is defined as the average size of the Sun during the year, make an estimate of how much larger or smaller the Sun might appear to be for each season. For example, if you think the Sun would be 25% larger in the summer, you would write in 125% in the space marked summer. If your students are not ready to work with percentages, you can ask them to use centimeters: if the average size of the Sun in pictures is about 10 cm across, how many centimeters across would the Sun be in pictures taken when the Sun is closest to Earth? When the Sun is farthest from Earth?

The ratio of **closest** Earth-Sun distance to the **farthest** Earth-Sun distance is about 97%.
Student worksheet is below—half sheet for photocopying two per page.

A version of this activity also appears on the CD-ROM (see page 56). Other images available on the CD-ROM: one solar image per month.

Sample Solar Diameter Measurements
The largest diameter measured was on the image taken on January 2.

Date	Diameter	Approximate Distance from Sun
1/2/97	10.3 cm	(Closest on Jan. 2) 147.1 million km
7/1/97	10.1 cm	(Farthest on July 4) 152.1 million km

Apparent Changes in the Sun's Size with Season

Instructions to the students

Images were taken of the Sun from an observatory in Hawaii at different seasons.
Place a ruler horizontally across each image and measure the largest distance across the middle of the Sun. Compare the measurements for each season. Images of the Sun were taken in Hawaii by Dr. Karen Mees of the University of Hawaii. Put your estimate in the table below.

Season	Size Estimate (compare to 100%)	Your Measurement
Winter		
Spring		
Summer		
Fall		

On what date is the Sun closest? _____

On what date is the Sun farthest?_____

Jan 1

Apr 1

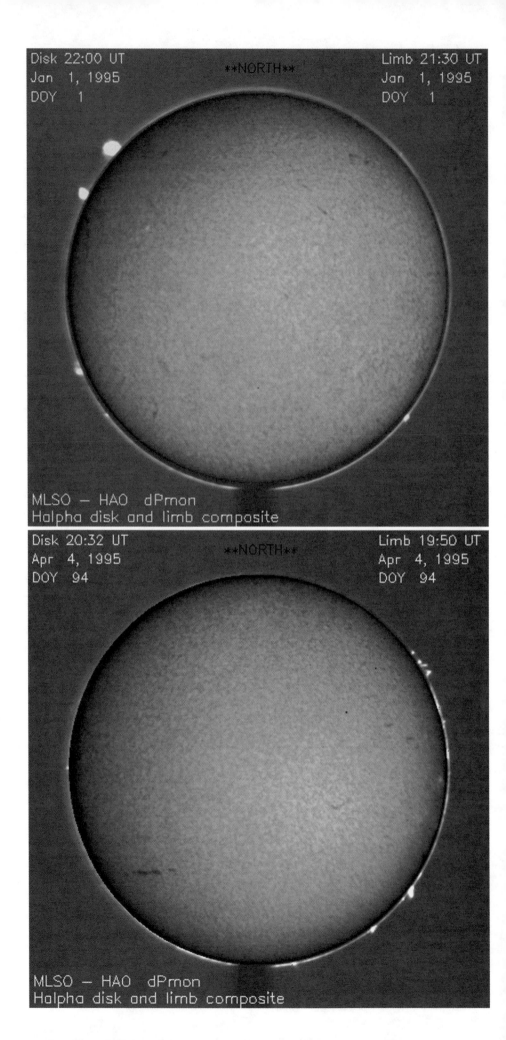

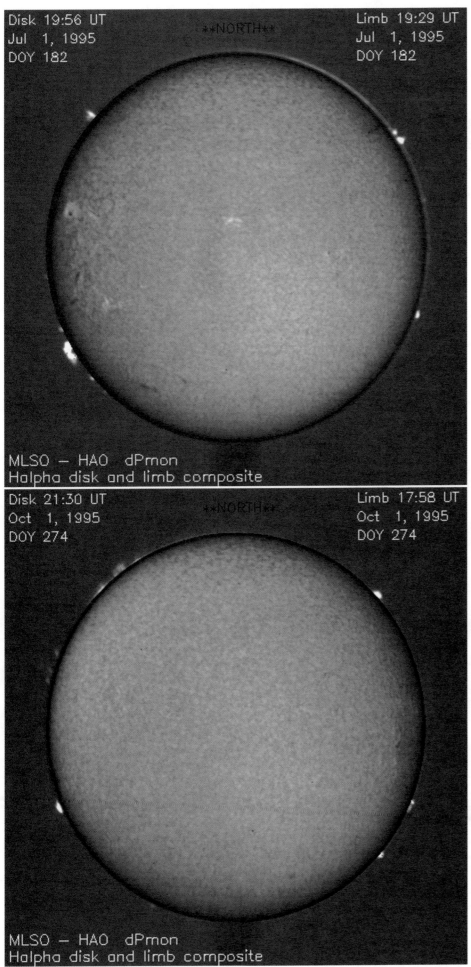

July 1

Oct 1

Get Out Your CD-ROM!

Student Worksheet: A similar activity to the one suggested in the "Going Further" on page 53 is also on the CD-ROM. The CD-ROM has images from the University of Hawaii's Mees Solar Observatory, taken each month, which can be used to compare the apparent size of the Sun throughout a year. Just go to the CD Home screen and click on the item under Activity 4: *Changes in the Sun's Size with the Season.*

This item on the CD-ROM also includes a link to a variety of solar images from Mount Wilson, an observatory near Los Angeles. These are images taken through special filters and ones that show the strength of magnetic fields at different places on the Sun. Such images help identify active and turbulent regions, such as those around sunspots.

There is also a link to the Nine Planets web site at SEDS (Students for the Exploration and Development of Space) at the University of Arizona, where you may readily find data on the orbits and eccentricities of the planets. Eccentricity is a measure of how elliptical an orbit can be. An eccentricity of 0 denotes a circular orbit. None of the orbits of the planets are exactly circular in shape. All are elliptical and some have significant eccentricity. Mathematically, eccentricity is defined as 1-(b/a) where a is the length of the semi-major axis and b is length of the semi-minor axis.

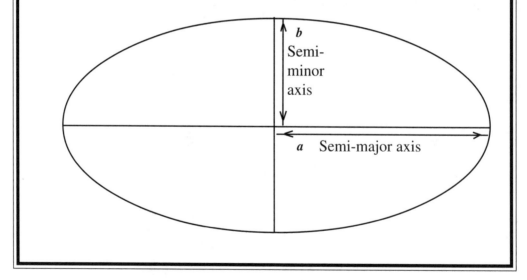

Activity 5: Temperatures Around the World

Overview

In this session, students analyze temperature data taken from the Globe project, a network of schools around the world dedicated to providing scientifically valid data on environmental characteristics related to weather, climate, and ecology.

In graphing the data, students discover interesting relationships in temperature changes—that the pattern of temperature change from summer to winter in one hemisphere is reversed with respect to the opposite hemisphere. This activity further dispels the idea that the Earth-Sun distance may be responsible for seasons.

What You Need

For each student:
- ❒ 1 List of locations with latitudes and longitudes (page 10 of Seasons Lab Book)
- ❒ 1 World Map (page 11 of Seasons Lab Book)
- ❒ 1 "Temperatures Around the World" data sheet (page 12 of Seasons Lab Book)
- ❒ 1 "Temperatures Around the World" graphing sheet (page 13 of Seasons Lab Book)
- ❒ 1 pencil

For each group of 4-6 students:
- ❒ 3–4 colored pens—assorted colors

For the class:
- ❒ 1 world globe
- ❒ 1 overhead transparency of World Map or a large World wall map (master in Seasons Lab Book, page 11)
- ❒ 1 overhead transparency of Temperature Data Sample (master in Getting Ready, next page)
- ❒ 1 overhead transparency of Temperatures Around the World Graph (blank; master in Seasons Lab Book, page 13)
- ❒ 1 overhead transparency of Temperature Around the World Graph (complete; master on page 59)
- ❒ 1 overhead projector
- ❒ 1 assortment of colored transparency pens

> ### Get Out Your CD-ROM!
>
> **Temperature Records**
> The changing seasons account for the variation in weather conditions and for extremes in temperature. On the CD-ROM is a listing of some of the temperature and weather records. Did you know, for example, that the coldest recorded temperature on Earth was -128.6° F (-89.2° C) on July 21, 1983, at Vostok station, Antarctica? For more, just go to the CD Home screen and click on the item under Activity 5: *Temperature Records*.

Getting Ready

1. Make an overhead transparency of the blank "Temperatures Around the World" graphing sheet (page 13 of the Lab Book) and the completed Temperature Graph (master on next page) and color code the temperature lines with colored transparency pens. Also make an overhead transparency of the Temperature Sample Data on the bottom of this page.

2. Check to see if your students understand how and are proficient at finding things on Earth by latitude and longitude. If not, try using some of the ideas in the "Behind the Scenes" background section (page 99) to strengthen students' skills.

Master for overhead transparency

Sample Data

Chalatenango, El Salvador
Escuela Rural Mixta
Latitude : 14°N
Longitude : 89°W
Elevation : 1700 m

Month	Year	Avg Temp
Oct	1997	16.9
Sep	1997	16.5
Aug	1997	16.3
Jul	1997	15.7
Jun	1997	15.7
May	1997	16.0
Apr	1997	15.3
Mar	1997	15.5
Feb	1997	15.4
Dec	1996	15.1

Temperatures Around the World

Label each temperature plot line according to latitude and state/country

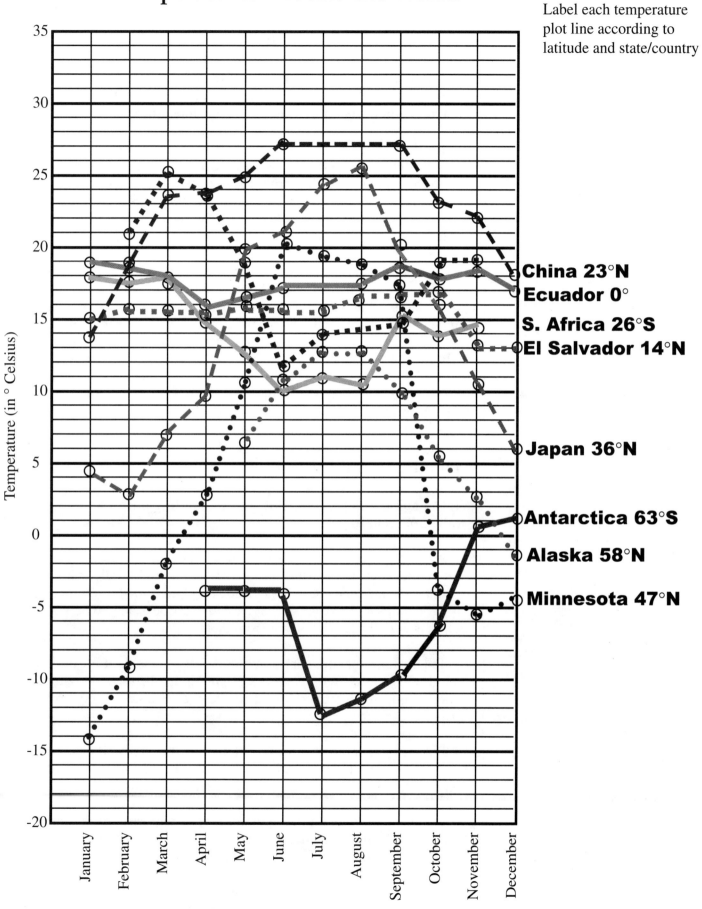

China 23°N
Ecuador 0°
S. Africa 26°S
El Salvador 14°N

Japan 36°N

Antarctica 63°S
Alaska 58°N
Minnesota 47°N

Temperatures Around the World

1. Ask students to think back to the "Name the Season" game, when they wrote about things that change with the seasons. Point out that one thing they mentioned often was the temperature.

2. Tell the class that students in many places around the world measure the temperature throughout a year, as part of an international environmental monitoring project known as Project Globe. Today, your students will get to see how those temperatures changed throughout the seasons, and how the patterns of change differ depending on where in the world you are.

3. Put the transparency with the data from El Salvador on the overhead projector. Say they will get this kind of information for each of nine places. Show how the data are arranged: the name of the city and country (Chalatenango, El Salvador); the name of the school whose students measured the temperature (Escuela Rural Mixta); the latitude (14°N), longitude (89°W), which tell where Chalatenango is located; the elevation, telling how high above sea level Chalatenango is (1700 meters). Next is a list of the average monthly temperatures. Emphasize that these are *monthly average temperatures*—not just the average for one day, but the average for a whole month.

Longitude and Latitude

1. Hold up the globe, and point out the *longitude* lines that run vertically from pole to pole.

2. Ask a volunteer to trace the equator on the globe. Explain that the set of lines that goes around the globe horizontally, parallel with the equator are *latitude* lines. The latitude and longitude lines form a grid on maps and globes, so that we can describe exactly where a place is with the two lines that cross there.

3. Tell the class that on maps and globes, each line of latitude and longitude is numbered in degrees. (*Optional:* Explain why longitude and latitude are described in angular degrees. See sidebar on next page.)

4. Put the transparency of the world map on the overhead projector. Again, point out the longitude lines running north-south, and the equator and other latitude lines running horizontally.

5. On the map, show that the equator is zero degrees latitude, and each latitude line to the north adds five degrees until the north pole, which is 90 degrees north latitude. Going south from the equator, each latitude also increases by 5 degrees, and the south pole is 90 degrees south. Emphasize the importance of saying **north** or **south** along with the number of degrees of latitude.

Students may notice that the average temperature data for January and November are missing for Chalatenango. This is what happens sometimes with real data. We did not receive information from the GLOBE schools for those two months.

Students can successfully do this activity with only the brief introduction to latitude and longitude that we have included. However, you may want to provide a fuller understanding of longitude and latitude.

Latitude lines are drawn horizontally, parallel to the equator. Latitude tells us how far a location is north or south of the equator. Longitude tells us how far a location is east or west of the prime meridian, which is the north-south line that runs through Greenwich, England and West Africa.

6. Point out that the longitude lines go from 0° to 180° and increase 5° to the east and west.

7. Demonstrate how to find Chalatenango, El Salvador on the world map using its latitude (14° north) and longitude (89° west).

8. Have the students locate, mark, and label the nine cities (page 10 of the Lab Book) on their world maps. Depending on your students' experience, give them ten minutes or more to do this. Go around and help as needed.

9. Ask early finishers to do some additional practice with a partner. Have one partner pick a place on the map, describe it only with the longitude and latitude, and see if their partner can find it.

Graphing Temperatures Around the World

1. Tell the class that they will look at the temperature during the year in the nine different places on Earth they have just located on their maps. Tell them that the data is on page 12 of their lab books.

2. Explain (or remind them) that scientists all over the world use the Celsius temperature scale. If students are used to the Fahrenheit scale, tell them there is a table on the left side of page 12 in their lab books that shows Celsius temperatures converted to Fahrenheit. Have students use the table to find the freezing point of water (the temperature at which water turns to ice or ice melts) in both scales [32°F or 0°C] What is a normal human temperature in each scale? [98.6°F or 37° C.]

The formula for converting temperatures from Fahrenheit to Celsius is $°C = (5/9) x (°F - 32)$.

3. Put the blank Temperature Graph transparency on the overhead projector. Demonstrate how to plot, for instance, a temperature average of 12°C in January. Point out that the lines on the graph are ~~two~~ one degree apart. Make sure students know what negative numbers mean, and how to plot temperatures that are below zero.

4. Ask, "What do you think the graph would look like in our area over the time period from January to June?" (Average temperature will rise.) "What would happen after that?" (Average temperature will fall.)

5. Ask, "Does the temperature have the same pattern as ours all over the world?" Explain that by graphing temperatures from several places around the world, they can find out if seasons differ in various locations.

You may want to point out the difference between the apparent size of Antarctica on the globe and on the flat map. The difference is due to map distortion resulting from the translation from the three-dimensional globe surface to the flat map.

Optional: Relate latitude and longitude to angles along the spherical surface of Earth. Along these lines it may be a good idea to review what angles are as follows:

1. Hold your arm out horizontally pointing towards something at eye level like a window or poster on the wall.

2. Sweep your arm through a full circle vertically. Ask, "How many degrees are in a full circle?" [360°]

3. Point to your original horizontal arm position and say "If we call this angle zero degrees ....
   then what angle is this?" (pointing arm straight up)

4. What angle is this (pointing 180° from starting/ 0° position)?

6. If your students need practice, plot the average temperatures for Chalatenango, El Salvador together on the overhead transparency. Then assign the students to plot average temperatures for as many cities as they can on the "Temperatures Around the World" graph (page 13 of lab book). It's not necessary for each student to graph all temperatures in all locations, though some really get into the process and gain a sense of great satisfaction when the whole job is done. It works well if the first two cities they plot are in opposite hemispheres—one in the Northern Hemisphere and one in the Southern Hemisphere. Here are a few different strategies to choose from.

    a. Have each student graph three cities: one Northern Hemisphere, on Southern Hemisphere, and one near the equator.

    b. Have each small group of students practice "division of labor," with each student taking two different cities to graph, but not necessarily the same ones as others in their group, so that by working together the group has a complete set of graphs.

    c. Assign various groups of students to pretend they are from the different cities. They start by graphing their own city's data and then move on to other cities. If they like, they can decide on their own strategy like moving to the closest cities first, or working their way north or south.

    d. Allow students to do more graphing at home for extra credit, or just for the sheer satisfaction of "job completion."

7. Tell students to connect the data points with a smooth line. If data are missing for any months, they should estimate where the plot line would go for those months. After plotting in pencil, they should trace over each line with a different color. Have them make a key by writing the color used, country name, and latitude on the right side of the graph. If they run out of colored pens, they can connect points with dashed or dotted lines, as a coding scheme. In some cases, the months do not run from January to December, but , for example, from July of one year to June of the next. Tell students not to worry about which year the month is in. Just be careful to plot the right average temperature to the right month of the year on the graph.

Analyzing the Temperature Graphs

1. After all students have plotted at least three cities on the graph, gather their attention, and ask, "What have we found out? " "What patterns do you see in your graphs?"

Optional: Have the students first discuss in small groups what the patterns are on their graphs, then report their findings in a whole class discussion.

Optional: Tell students they can earn extra credit in this unit for doing an analysis of how the sunrise and sunset positions change with the seasons. There is more about this at the end of this session.

2. Make sure students notice that the pattern is reversed between the Northern and Southern Hemispheres. In the Northern Hemisphere, hottest months are June-August, while in the Southern Hemisphere, hottest months are December-February. Ask, "What season is it where we live in July?" (Summer.) "What season is it in Antarctica in July?" (Winter.)

3. Ask, "What is the pattern of temperature change for locations near the equator?" [There is not much variation in temperature through all the seasons.]

4. Remind students of question #3 in the Sun-Earth Survey. Ask them what they think of answer B in light of what they have observed on their global temperature graphs.

> *Note: the two cities in Ecuador each do not have complete annual data. Together, they might span all months of the year, but notice their elevations: one is near sea level and the other is at 1,700 meters (5,577 feet). Although there is not much seasonal temperature variation for each city, it is interesting that overall the higher elevation city is much cooler.*

Get Out Your CD-ROM!

Seasons: Alaska, Australia, and Antarctica

An Unusual Beginning to Spring in Alaska

How do you tell when Spring has arrived? In central Alaska a contest has been held for over 80 years to predict the breakup of ice in the Tatana River. The Tatana River freezes over during October and November and the ice usually breaks up in late April or early May. The exact time may be used to sense changes in climate. More information is found via web link on the CD-ROM.

Australia Seasonal Change Movies for 1981-1990

Have you ever wondered what the change of seasons looks like in Australia? Satellite images show seasonal changes over several years for all of Australia. The satellite data have been made into a movie that shows the amount of vegetation. You can watch movies of Australia's seasons from 1981-1990 at a web site on the CD-ROM.

Seasons in the Antarctic: The Bancroft Arnesen Expedition

In November 2000, Ann Bancroft and Liv Arnesen will fly to Antarctica, accompanied by only their skis, two sleds, and enough food and equipment for their 100-day, 2,400-mile (3,850 km) trek across Antarctica. If they successfully complete their traverse in February 2001, they will be the first all-women's team to cross Antarctica. Their expedition will be broadcast over the Internet to a hoped-for audience of 3 million students.

There is also information on current Antarctic weather through the Antarctic Connection weather information web pages.

To get to any of these websites, just go to the CD Home screen and click on the item under Activity 5: *Seasons: Alaska, Australia, and Antarctica.*

Get Out Your CD-ROM!

Journey North

The Journey North is a web-based project to track animal migration in the spring. Over 4,500 schools, representing approximately 200,000 students, take part. These students come from all 50 U.S. States and 7 Canadian Provinces. Journey North is a free online educational service, supported by the Annenberg/CPB Math and Science Project.

"The journeys of a dozen migratory species are tracked each spring. Students share their own field observations with classrooms across the Hemisphere. In addition, students are linked with scientists who provide their expertise directly to the classroom. Several migrations are tracked by satellite telemetry, providing live coverage of individual animals as they migrate. As the spring season sweeps across the Hemisphere, students note changes in daylight, temperatures, and all living things as the food chain comes back to life."

Just go to the CD Home screen and click on the item under Activity 5: *Journey North.*

Activity 6: Days and Nights Around the World

Overview

By graphing the number daylight hours per day in cities around the world, students find a very symmetrical pattern of daylight hours that is exactly opposite for the Southern and Northern Hemispheres. Students discover months when the Sun never sets in Alaska, and never rises in Antarctica. They also discover the meaning of the equinoxes, as they find day and night hours are equal in September and March everywhere on Earth.

As in the prior session, graphing and reflecting on these interesting data can help give students a global perspective, and should prepare them to better understand the explanations for the seasons brought together in Activity 8.

It may seem like a lot of graphing to have this activity and the one before it, back to back. But we have seen great benefits resulting from this practice. One student, who initially had great difficulties graphing the temperatures and was the "slowest" in the class, experienced a breakthrough in this second graphing exercise and miraculously finished these graphs among the first in the class!

This activity focuses on seasonal variations in day length, and not the Sun's position in the sky from sunrise to sunset. If you would like your students to also explore seasonal changes in the Sun's position, see Going Further Activity #2 outlined at the end of this session, with student sheets in the back of the guide.

What You Need

For each student:
- ❒ 1 "Seasonal Changes in Day Length" data sheet (page 14 of Seasons Lab Book)
- ❒ 1 "Day Length" graphing sheet (page 15 of Seasons Lab Book)
- ❒ 1 pencil

For each group of 4-6 students:
- ❒ 3–4 colored pens—assorted colors

For the class:
- ❒ 1 transparency of Day Length Data Sample (master in Getting Ready; on bottom half of next page, page 66)
- ❒ 1 transparency of World Map or a large World wall map (master in Season Lab Book, page 11)
- ❒ 1 transparency of Day Length Graph (blank; master in Seasons Lab Book, page 15)
- ❒ 1 transparency of Day Length Graph (complete; master on page 67 in teacher's guide)
- ❒ Optional: photograph of a sunset

Getting Ready

1. Make an overhead transparency of the blank Day Length Graph (page 15 of the Lab Book).

2. Make an overhead transparency of the completed Day Length Graph (master on page 67 of teacher's guide) and color code the lines with colored pens.

3. Make an overhead transparency of the sample "Day Length" data on the bottom half of this page.

Seasonal Changes in DAY LENGTH

All dates are the 21st day of the month.

Sample Data

Latitude: 38° North

Date	Sunrise (AM)	Sunset (PM)	Day Length (hours)
Jan	7:22	5:21	9:59
Feb	6:52	5:55	11:03
Mar	6:12	6:23	12:11
Apr	5:26	6:51	13:25
May	4:55	7:18	14:23
Jun	4:47	7:36	14:49
Jul	5:04	7:28	14:24
Aug	5:30	6:55	13:25
Sep	5:57	6:08	12:11
Oct	6:24	5:24	11:00
Nov	6:57	4:54	9:57
Dec	7:22	4:54	9:32

All the following cities are at about 38 degrees North latitude:

San Francisco, California
Charleston, W. Virginia
Wichita, Kansas
St. Louis, Missouri
Louisville, Kentucky
Pueblo, Colorado
Richmond, Virginia
Sendai, Japan   Athens, Greece
Seoul, S. Korea   Palermo, Sicily
Tientsin, China   Cordoba, Spain
Izmir, Turkey   Lisbon, Portugal

7. Days and Nights Around the World: Seasonal Changes in Number of Hours of Daylight

Label each plot line:
a. latitude and
b. state/country

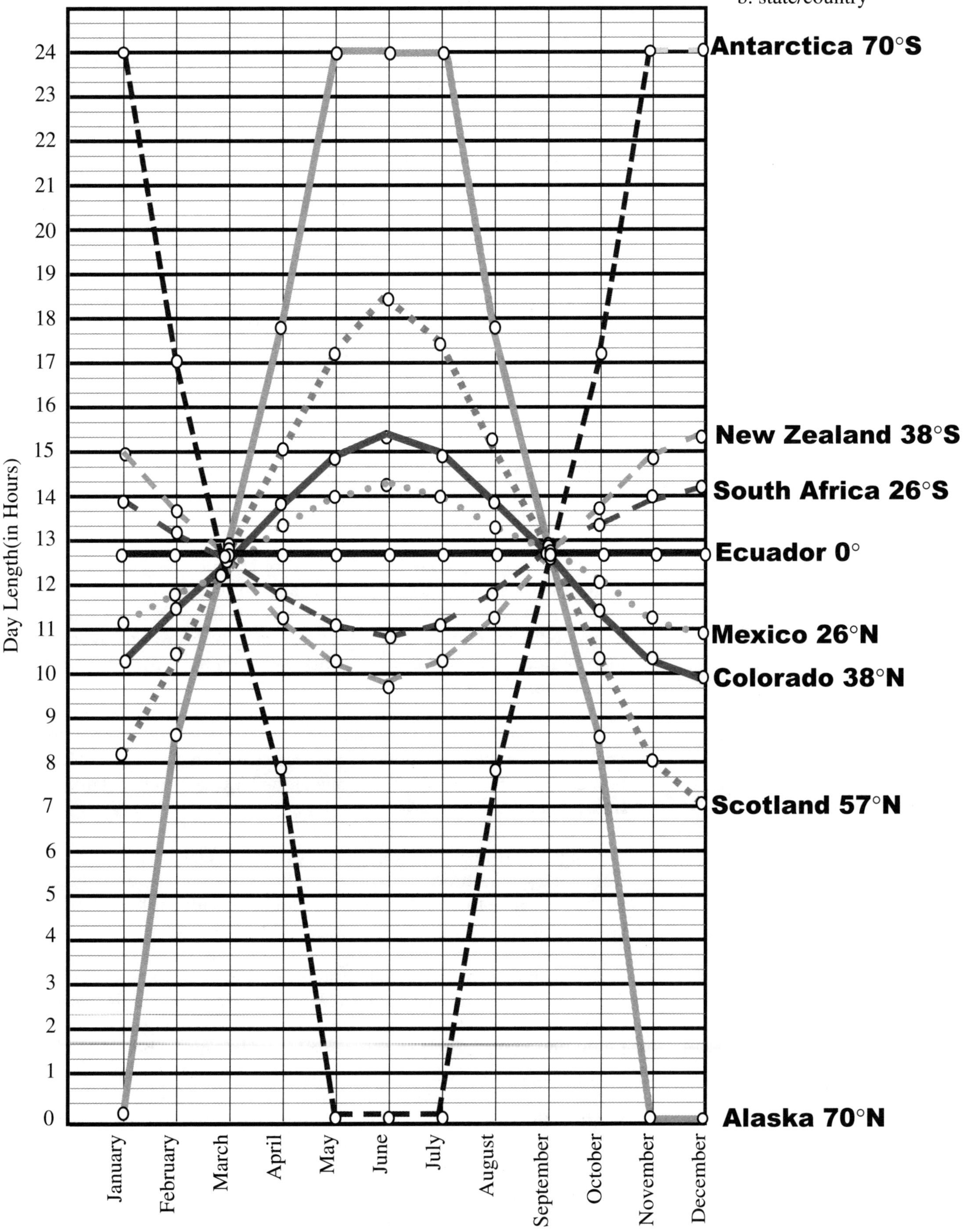

Day Length(in Hours)
0
1
2
3
4
5
6
7
8
9
10
11
12
13
14
15
16
17
18
19
20
21
22
23
24
January
February
March
April
May
June
July
August
September
October
November
December
Antarctica 70°S
New Zealand 38°S
South Africa 26°S
Ecuador 0°
Mexico 26°N
Colorado 38°N
Scotland 57°N
Alaska 70°N

Hours of Daylight

We will sometimes refer to the number of hours of daylight as "length of day," even though technically a day is the time it takes Earth to spin once, which is always approximately 24 hours (23 hours and 56 minutes).

1. Have the students again think back to Activity 1, when they wrote about changes that occur with the seasons. Ask how many of them wrote about changes in the "length of day."

2. To review their experience with changes in the number of daylight hours, ask the following questions:

- Does the Sun always set at the same time each day? [No] Optional: show a photograph of a sunset to add a vivid element to this discussion.

- At what times of year does the Sun stay up latest (and rise the earliest)? [Summer. Don't reveal the answer if no one knows.]

- Is the number of hours of daylight the same each day?" [No]

- When are the "shortest days?" [Winter]

3. Ask, "Is the number of hours of daylight on a certain day the same all over the world?" Tell the students that in this session, they will look at day length data from different places around the world.

4. Show the sample "Day Length" data for Latitude 38 degrees north on the overhead projector. Explain what each column means: sunrise time, sunset time, and "Day Length," which is the number of actual hours of daylight on the 21st day of each month. Show on a world map or globe how all the cities in this list are on the same latitude, 38 degrees north.

5. Explain that these data are on page 14 of the lab book, along with data for seven other latitudes, with some cities listed for each. Model how to graph the day length for one of the latitudes on the blank graph transparency.

6. Assign the students to graph as many of the "Day Length" values from the eight latitudes as they can on the graphs on page 15 of their lab books. Have them color code the plot lines with a different color for each latitude.

7. Tell them that the first two latitudes they plot should be in opposite hemispheres: one in the Southern Hemisphere and one in the Northern Hemisphere. For students who are not as proficient at graphing, you might hint that a latitude near 0° (e.g., Ecuador) might be a particularly easy place to start.

8. Allow the students to continue graphing as long as possible, but leave at least ten minutes for a discussion. Try to be sure all students have finished graphing at least three or four of the eight latitudes before the discussion.

Discussing the "Day Length" Graphs

1. Regain the attention of the class.

2. Tell them that you have prepared a graph that should look something like theirs. Put the "Day Length" graph transparency on the overhead projector. Ask, "What patterns do you see?" (Optional: have students discuss in small groups and then share their views in a whole class discussion.)

3. Point to the Ecuador data, and ask, "If the data make a straight horizontal line across the graph, what does that say about how the length of day changes at that latitude?" [Day length stays the same all year.] Ask, "What do the lines that go up and down steeply tell you?" [At that latitude, day length changes greatly with the seasons.]

4. Be sure that students notice that locations at opposite latitudes in northern and Southern Hemispheres have day lengths which are mirror images of each other. Ask, "What season is it in Scotland in July?" [summer] "What season is it in New Zealand in July?" [winter] Students should be able to perceive that there is a high degree of symmetry: Moreover, each plot line is highly symmetrical on either side of the month of June.

5. Ask, "Are there any places where the Sun never comes up (zero day length) in certain parts of the year?" [Yes. Antarctica, Alaska, Norway, Canada.] At what times of year does that happen? [It happens at opposite times of the year in the far north and far south. The Sun never comes up from November through January at latitudes north of 70° N. From May through July, the Sun never comes up at latitudes south of 70°S latitude.]

6. "Where and when does the Sun stay up for 24 hours?" [The Sun never sets from May through July above 70°N latitude (Alaska); also November through January at latitudes south of 70° S.(Antarctica) This is sometimes called the "midnight Sun."]

7. If no one points out that all the lines converge at two points, ask, "Are there any places where all the lines come together?" [Yes, in March and September] "What seasons are in March and September?" [spring and fall, respectively]

8. Explain that there is a special name for the exact date where all the lines come together, when the number of hours of daylight equals the number of hours of night time. Ask if anyone knows what those special days are called. [*Equinoxes*—Spring equinox and fall or autumnal equinox] They occur near March 21 and September 21 each year.

Ask if any of your students have ever visited or lived in a place with very different day lengths than those in your school's region. If time permits, allow some discussion of what it must be like to have no daylight or no darkness for 24 hours.

9. Remind students of question #3 in the Sun-Earth Survey. Ask, "Do your observations about the number of daylight hours help you rule out any of the answers?"

10. Tell the class the next activity will make clear for them why the day length changes with the seasons the way it does.

Going Further

1. Devise a Seasons Card Game. Each card could give a clue much like the ones students wrote in Activity 1, except now, the clues can include global season information. Have students make a pile of season clue cards with equal numbers of cards for each season. Then, in turn, students draw cards from the pile, trying to make matching pairs. The winner is the one with the most matching pairs. For example, these two cards could form a pair for *spring*:

"The kangaroos are everywhere, now that it's October."
"I saw the Sun today for the first time in months here in northern Alaska."
                    (In this case, the two "springs" are six months apart!)

Please Note: Data sheets for this "Going Further" activity can be found in the back of this guide, just after "Behind the Scenes," on pages 100–104. Some additional information appears on page 99.

2. Seasonal Changes in Sun Position. Another important seasonal change that students can explore is the variation in where the Sun rises and sets, and its elevation in the sky at noon. If you would like to give your students a homework/extra credit opportunity, challenge them to plot those data and summarize patterns that they find. In the back of the guide, pages 100–104, you'll find data sheets for:

  (a) Sunset position (azimuth angle)
  (b) Sunrise position (azimuth angle)
  (c) Noon position (altitude or elevation angle)

  Note: The noon position is especially relevant to explaining how the angle of sunlight affects seasons. This relationship is also explored through the models used in the next two activities.

Students can plot data on the three charts: "Sunset Positions," "Sunrise Positions," and "Sun Elevation Angles." On page 104 is a chart for drawing the path of the Sun on a single day—students can mark sunrise azimuth angle, noon elevation angle, and sunset asimuth angle on a particular day, then draw in the arc that is the approximate path of the Sun throughout that day.

Calculating the Position of the Sun

Where is the Sun in the sky at a particular time and day? A Sun angle calculator is used by architects designing solar heated buildings and by others who need to be able to predict the Sun's position. On a Sun angle calculator you set the latitude of your position, and the day and time. The calculator will tell you the elevation of the Sun, and its angle from north, or azimuth.

There are several Sun angle calculators included or described on the CD-ROM. First is the program Starry Night, which allows you to notice the position of the Sun (or Moon and stars) at any time, for any particular location on Earth. It even allows you to go back or forward in time to look. Starry Night can be used to produce information on sunrise/sunset positions and times for any location on Earth. A step by step guide for those teachers unfamiliar with the program is included on the CD-ROM.

There are also programs on the web which allow you to find the position of the Sun. To access these resources, just go to the CD Home screen and click on the item under Activity 6:
Calculating the Position of the Sun.

Architect Sun Angle Calculator
There are also cardboard "calculators" used by architects which allow you to predict the Sun's position. The best known example was made by Libby Owens Ford (a glass company) and is available for $10 (check only) from Ms. Kathy Raszka/Libby Owens Ford, 811 Madison Ave., Toledo Ohio 43697, phone (419) 247-3731

Solar Motion Demonstrator
There is also a very useful device called the Solar Motion Demonstrator that is available from the Astronomical Society of the Pacific (ASP). The device accurately models the motion of the Sun as seen from any place in the Northern Hemisphere at any time of year. On the ASP web site (http://www.aspsky.org/) there are many excellent resources, including a description by Joseph L. Snider of ways to use the Solar Motion Demonstrator. The ASP catalog sells kits of 25 Solar Motion Dectectors.

Activity 7: Tilted Earth

Overview

Having explored the distance to the Sun, the shape of the Earth's orbit, and the differing temperatures and day lengths around the world, your class is ready to gain a deeper and more scientifically accurate and complete understanding of what causes the seasons.

Using small polystyrene spheres or Earth globes as model "Earths," with a light-bulb as a model "Sun," students create a model that shows how the tilt of the Earth's spin axis causes seasons. This model is especially effective in showing what causes seasonal variations in daylength.

What You Need

For the class:
- ❐ 32 polystyrene balls
- ❐ 32 pencils
- ❐ 100 watt bulb with clip-on socket and extension cord
- ❐ Optional: 8 Earth globes

Getting Ready

1. For this activity, you will need to darken the room. If your room is difficult to darken, you may need to try to borrow a resource or other room that can be darkened.

2. Set up the light bulb above eye level near the center of the room. You may want to clip the light to a box on top of a cart or table. The bulb needs to be clearly visible to all the students when they form a circle around it.

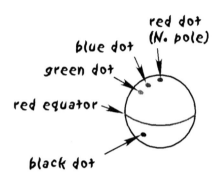

3. Mark the polystyrene balls with different colored, indelible felt-tipped markers as follows:

    a. Draw a line to represent the equator in one color (red)

    b. Make a large dot in the same color (red) at the "North Pole" of the ball.

    c. Make a dot roughly halfway from the equator to the pole using the color green. This will represent a mid-latitude city like San Francisco or your home town if that applies.

    d. Make a second dot in the color blue at a latitude of roughly 70°, i.e. closer to the pole than the equator. This will represent a far northerly locale such as Trömso, Norway or Prudhoe Bay, Alaska.

    e. Make one more dot (black) halfway from the equator to the South Pole to represent a mid-latitude Southern Hemisphere city like Melbourne, Australia.

Introducing the Model

1. Ask students to remember the shape of the Earth's orbit that they drew in Activity 3. [almost circular] Does the Earth's distance from the Sun change very much during the year? [no]

2. Point out that if the Earth did move closer or farther from the Sun, it would be colder or hotter everywhere on Earth at the same time. Ask, "Is it summer at the same time everywhere on Earth? [No—in the last two activities, we found that summer and winter happen at the same time on different parts of the world.]

3. Ask, "If it is not the distance to the Sun that causes seasons, what are some other possible causes?" [It may have something to do with the direction the Earth is tilted.] If a student mentions this idea, proceed, otherwise, mention it yourself.

4. Tell the class that they will make a Sun-Earth model to explain the seasons, with the Sun represented by a light bulb. This time, instead of their heads representing the Earth, they will each get a polystyrene sphere to represent the Earth. Show them how to put the sphere on a pencil to spin it. Say that this represents how the Earth rotates on a "spin axis" that runs roughly from the north to the South Pole.

5. Caution the students to be respectful and quiet during the activity so that everyone can hear and understand your directions. Also caution them not to write on or otherwise damage the spheres.

A Model with No Tilt

1. Hand out the model Earths. Have each student put a pencil into the hole in the sphere. Gather everyone in a circle around the light bulb, and turn off the lights in the rest of the room.

2. Ask students to find the Equator and the North Pole on their spheres, and the Northern and Southern Hemispheres. Identify the other three marks:

> • The green dot represents a mid-latitude location in the Northern Hemisphere (like most places in the continental US).

> • The blue dot represents a high-latitude location (like northern Alaska) in the Northern Hemisphere.

> • The black dot represents a mid-latitude location in the Southern Hemisphere, such as Melbourne, Australia.

3. First, have the students to hold their Earth models with the spin axis (pencil) vertical, slowly spin them, and watch their dot cities move from daylight into night and back again. Ask, "With your pencil (spin axis) vertical, do the blue, green, and black dots stay in the light the same amount of time (daytime)?" [Yes, roughly]

4. Ask, "Is this really how the Sun-Earth system works?" [No. The spin axis should be tilted.] Instruct everyone to tilt the Earth towards the Sun in the model—not with the pole pointing directly towards the Sun, but tilted roughly halfway down (45° angle). The real angle is 23.5°, but let's exaggerate for now.

5. Instruct the students to spin the Earth again and watch the dots. Ask them to compare what is happening at the green dot and black dot cities (mid-latitude north and Southern Hemisphere) Do they both get day and night? [yes, but the city in the Northern Hemisphere has long days and short nights, while in the Southern Hemisphere, there are long nights and short days.]

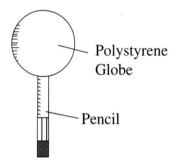

Polystyrene Globe

Pencil

Students should spin stheir "Earths" in a counter-clockwise direction, as seen from above. Later on, when the students circle around the Sun, they will be moving in a counter-clockwise direction. This is an accurate reflection of the astronomical fact that the spin of the Earth on its axis goes in the same direction as its revolution around the Sun.

6. Ask, "How about the blue dot—does it have day and night?" [No. It receives light the whole 24 hours; it has midnight Sun.] What is happening near the South Pole? [24 hours of darkness]

7. Have students compare what is happening in the two Northern Hemisphere cities. Ask, what season is it in the green dot city? The blue dot? [both have summer] How are they different? [The day length is longer in the blue dot city.]

8. Say that all their Northern Hemispheres are tilted toward the Sun, and have summer. Is this how it always is? How does the season change from summer to fall, winter, and spring during the year? Does the Earth rock back and forth? [no]

Tilting the Earth Toward the North Star

1. Tell the students that, as the Earth moves around the Sun, **the North Pole always points at the North Star.**

2. Pick a spot in the classroom to represent the North Star, e.g. the clock or a poster mounted high on a wall. Ideally, make your model North Star in the direction of the real North Star. Ask all the students to tilt the North Pole of their spheres toward the North Star. Have them practice spinning the spheres while keeping the North Pole pointed at the North Star.

3. Go around to check that students standing between the Sun and the North Star are keeping their North Poles tilted *away* **from the Sun**, and toward the North Star. Students standing on the opposite side of the "orbit" should have their North Poles **tilted** *toward* **the Sun** (and the North Star). Students midway between these positions will have the North Pole pointing "sideways" to the Sun.

The Earth's north spin axis points almost exactly towards the North Star (within a degree). That is why the North Star always stays at the same spot in the sky while all the other stars seem to "revolve around it."

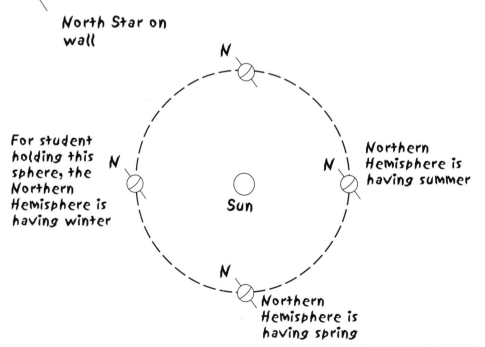

North Star on wall

For student holding this sphere, the Northern Hemisphere is having winter

Sun

Northern Hemisphere is having summer

Northern Hemisphere is having spring

4. Stand near the part of the class whose North Poles are tilted towards the Sun. Ask, "When the Earth is in this part of its orbit, which Hemisphere is tilted more towards the Sun?" [Northern.] "Is it the same season in both Northern and Southern Hemispheres?" [No. In the Northern Hemisphere, it's summer, and in the Southern Hemisphere it's winter.]

5. Move **counterclockwise** (as seen from above) around the circle of students stopping at 3 positions: 1/4 of the way around, halfway around and 3/4 of the way around. At each stop, ask, "For the model Earths in this part of the orbit, is the North Pole pointing towards the Sun or away from the Sun?" [At the 1/4 and 3/4 stops the answer is neither—it's pointing "sideways" to the Sun.] "What season is this?" [1st stop it's fall in Northern Hemisphere; spring in Southern Hemisphere; 2nd stop it's winter in Northern Hemisphere and summer in Southern Hemisphere; 3rd stop it's spring in the Northern Hemisphere and fall in the Southern Hemisphere.]

As noted earlier, to accurately model what really takes place, students should spin their globes in a counterclockwise direction, as seen from above.

6. Point to the students you started out with, who have North Poles tilted toward the Sun—the Northern Hemisphere's summer position. Ask, "If Norway and Alaska are watching the midnight Sun, what are folks seeing in Antarctica?" (Stars—24-hour nights.)

7. Review by asking students to raise their hands if their Earth position has:

- longer days at the South Pole.
- longer days at the North Pole.
- day length is about the same in both Hemispheres.

8. Ask students to rotate their model Earths until their "hometown" (the green dot) is at noontime. Ask, "Can you tell in which season the Sun gets highest in the sky at noon?" [summer]

9. Collect the spheres, turn on the room lights, and have the students return to their seats.

Discussing the Model and What Causes Seasons

1. Ask students to write down on paper what they learned about the causes of seasons. Give them four or five minutes to do this, then ask a few volunteers to explain what they learned from the model.

2. Ask, "Do you think a planet whose axis was not tilted at all would have seasons?" [No.]

3. Say that many people think that the tilt of the Earth causes seasons because it makes one part of the Earth much closer to the Sun. Ask, "When the North Pole is tilted toward the Sun, is the Northern Hemisphere much closer to the Sun than the Southern Hemisphere?" [No—a few thousand kilometers is not significant compared with the nearly 15 million kilometers distance from the Earth to the Sun.]

4. Remind them of their scale model in Activity 3—if the Earth were the size of a pinhead, the Sun would be a 28 cm beach ball thirty meters away. Ask, "Does it make much difference in the 30 meter distance to the Sun if the pinhead is tilted?" [no] Emphasize that the distance from the Earth to the Sun is enormous—much greater than in the light-bulb model they just used.

5. If the tilt doesn't make much difference in our distance from the Sun, why does it get hotter in summer? [There are more hours of daylight. It's the angle of the sunlight that makes the light more concentrated in summer, **but don't reveal this yet unless a student mentions it.**] Tell students that in the next session, the class will explore that question.

6. Refer to question #3 on the Seasons Survey. Ask which answers are supported by the model they just made.

> *If the Northern Hemisphere is tilted towards the Sun, technically it is closer to the Sun than the Southern Hemisphere. But it is closer to the Sun by a distance that is less than the diameter of Earth which is 12,750 km. This is negligible when compared with the overall distance to the Sun which is 149,600,000 km. You might want to have your students calculate the % difference.*

Optional: Play the Seasons-Orbit Game

1. Define these hand symbols for the four seasons:
   a. Winter, students hold up closed fist in front of their faces, representing seeds waiting to sprout.
   b. Spring, students put open their hands in front of their faces, representing sprouting plants.
   c. Summer, students raise their hands high in the air, representing fully grown plants.
   d. Fall, students let their hands fall down to their sides, representing falling leaves.

2. Now add the revolution of the Earth around the Sun. Have the students walk around (orbit) the Sun. Tell them to make sure the axis of their Earth **ALWAYS** points to the North Star.

3. Have students stop when they've gone 1/4 of the way around the circle. Check that the axes are still pointing to the North Star. Have students hold up the hand symbol for the season they are in now.

4. Repeat step 3 two more times so students have a chance to give the hand symbol for each season, making a complete annual cycle. Ask for questions or other ideas for ways to model the seasons.

Get Out Your CD-ROM!

Demonstration of the Seasons Game

On the CD-ROM look at the movie "Demonstration of the Seasons Game." This movie illustrates the movement of the Earth around the Sun in the Seasons game. Notice that as each student goes around the "Sun" the Earth's axis is pointed in a fixed direction in the room. The Earth's axis always points to a fixed point in space. In this way the Earth acts like a gyroscope or spinning top. The North Pole of the Earth's axis of rotation points to the North Star, Polaris.

To see the movies, just go to the CD Home screen and click on the item under Activity 1: *Demonstration of the Seasons Game.*

Get Out Your CD-ROM!

Seasons Software

The *Seasons* software, developed by Riverside Scientific, Inc., located at Augsburg College in Minneapolis, Minnesota, is a powerful modeling system that allows you to change the Earth's orbit and the tilt of the Earth's axis and then predict how these changes will affect the seasons. Riverside has developed several earth science software programs (*Seasons, Winds, Clouds*) that promote hands-on, inquiry-based learning. The programs were originally developed for exhibit kiosks in science centers and have proven to be engaging exhibits.

We include a time-trial version on this CD-ROM and encourage teachers and schools to buy the complete product, which includes a teacher's guide and student logbook. The software is available in either a Mac or PC version and at the time of this printing was $50 for an individual copy. Full details and trial versions of the other programs are available at the Riverside Scientific web site. Just go to the CD Home screen and click on the item under Activity 7: *Seasons Software.*

We encourage purchase of this program because its value to this unit and to student comprehension is large. Students can see for themselves the effect of the tilt of the Earth's axis on seasons. The program also shows how the amount of sunlight and the temperature of different places on Earth affects the seasons.

Activity 8: The Angle of Sunlight and Seasons Unraveled

Overview

Students have now seen how the tilt of the Earth causes day length to change with the seasons. In this closing activity and discussion, they are able to see more clearly how the Earth's tilt also changes **the angle at which the sunlight hits the ground**. In winter, rays of sunlight strike the ground at a slant and are **less** concentrated than the more perpendicular rays of the summer months. Using a "Sun Angle Analyzer" students explore and model this aspect.

Then, equipped with understandings gained from all their investigations, students revisit the Sun-Earth Survey, focusing first on question #3. They summarize the elements they've found that help explain the causes of seasons. The closing discussion brings home the fact that the Earth is a spinning globe whose axis **tilts** with respect to its orbit around the Sun, and this gives rise to: (a) a varying number of daylight hours in different seasons, and (b) variations in concentration of sunlight on the ground related to the angle the light strikes the ground. These are the main factors that cause seasons and since they stem from the relation between the Sun and the Earth, they are considered a "Sun-Earth connection."

What You Need

For each pair of students:
- ❏ 1 piece of scrap paper or the back of the Seasons Lab Book
- ❏ 1 Sun Angle Analyzer (master for photocopying on page 82)
- ❏ one paper fastener (or brad) with flat head
- ❏ pencil
- ❏ (Optional) a short piece of tape, any kind

For the class:
- ❏ 100 watt bulb with clip-on socket and extension cord
- ❏ 1 Earth globe—at least 20 cm (8") diameter
- ❏ (Optional) 1 small paper doll cutout or model action figure—not more than a few centimeters tall
- ❏ small piece of tape—almost any kind

Getting Ready

1. Set up the 100 watt light as in the previous activity.

2. Photocopy the Sun Angle Analyzers onto heavy cardstock. Prepare them by cutting them out along the dashed lines, including the small window, and folding along the dotted lines. The first time you do this unit, you can have students cut an fold the analyzers. Then for subsequent classes, the job is already done.

3. Familiarize yourself with how to use the Sun Angle Analyzer as described in step 4.

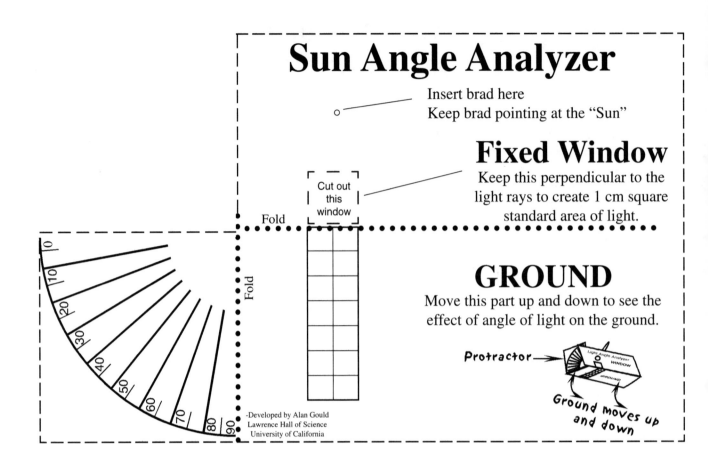

Sun Angle Analyzer

Insert brad here
Keep brad pointing at the "Sun"

Fixed Window
Keep this perpendicular to the
light rays to create 1 cm square
standard area of light.

Fold

Cut out
this
window

GROUND
Move this part up and down to see the
effect of angle of light on the ground.

Protractor →

Ground moves up
and down

-Developed by Alan Gould
Lawrence Hall of Science
University of California

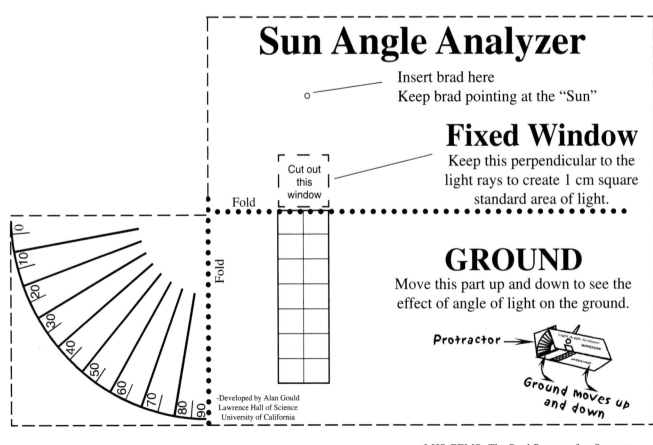

Sun Angle Analyzer

Insert brad here
Keep brad pointing at the "Sun"

Fixed Window
Keep this perpendicular to the
light rays to create 1 cm square
standard area of light.

Cut out
this
window

Fold

GROUND
Move this part up and down to see the
effect of angle of light on the ground.

Protractor →

Ground moves up
and down

-Developed by Alan Gould
Lawrence Hall of Science
University of California

The Angle of Sunlight

1. Tell the class that they already understand more about the seasons than many college graduates, but there is one more issue they need to consider before they can be considered experts on seasons. Explain that now they are going to look more carefully at how high the Sun appears in the sky during different seasons.

2. Turn on the light bulb-model Sun or use a point on the chalkboard or wall to represent the Sun. Hold up the class globe, and point out your location in the Northern Hemisphere. Tilt the Northern Hemisphere towards the Sun. Review, "What season is it where we live?" [summer] Spin the globe so your location is facing the Sun. "What time is it?" [noon]

3. Keep the Earth in the summer noon position for your location. Hold up a ruler. Say that it represents a ray of sunlight coming from the Sun to Earth during our summertime. Explain that light travels in a straight line. Place one end of the ruler on your location, and point the other end toward the Sun. (The ruler should hit the globe at a nearly perpendicular angle, as in the right-hand side of the drawing below.) Ask, "To someone at this point on Earth, would the Sun appear high in the sky or low in the sky?"

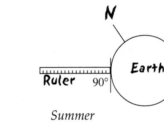

N
Ruler
Shallow angle
Earth
Winter

Sun

N
Ruler 90° *Earth*
Summer

4. Ask how the Earth is tilted when it's winter. Walk to the other side of the Sun and tilt the Northern Hemisphere away from the Sun, but spin it so your location is facing the Sun. Point out that the angle at which the ruler "sunlight ray" strikes the globe is now at a very shallow angle. (As in the left-hand side of the above drawing.)

5. Help students see that the Sun would seem to be overhead in the summer, but lower in the sky in winter. For each position, ask, "Where in the sky does the Sun seem to be?" [high overhead at noon in summer, lower in the sky at noon in winter]

Insert fastener through hole above window

Point of fastener

Introducing the Sun Angle Analyzer

1. Tell the students that they get to use a "Sun Angle Analyzer" to see what happens when light hits the ground at different angles.

2. Demonstrate how to stick a paper fastener (brad) through the x-mark just above the "window" hole. Poke it through from the printed side of the paper, so that the point sticks out on the blank side of the paper. Tape the head of the fastener down on the x to help keep it perpendicular to the Window. Tell students not to open the two prongs of the fastener, but to leave them closed. The fastener prongs will serve as a "pointer."

3. Explain that they'll use the analyzer with a partner. Hand out a Sun Angle Analyzer and a fastener to each pair of students. Once they have their fasteners in place, have them all gather around the light bulb. Turn off the room lights and close the blinds if possible.

4. Ignoring the protractor part for now, practice using the analyzers together. Call their attention to the instructions written on the Sun Angle Analyzers.

Keep the brad pointed at the "Sun"

a. Partner #1 holds the Window portion of the Analyzer and keeps it so that the standard, one-square-centimeter "Window" area stays perpendicular to the light rays. If the Window is allowed to stray significantly away from perpendicular, the area of light going through the window will no longer be the standard 1 square centimeter. The brad helps since, when the brad points directly to the light bulb, it does not cast a shadow. If the brad casts a shadow, you need to tilt the analyzer a bit until there is no shadow, making the standard, one-square-centimeter area window again perpendicular to the light rays. Give students time to play with the anayzers to see how this works.

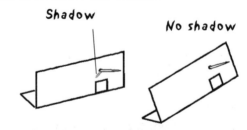

Shadow

No shadow

Get Out Your CD-ROM!

Pointing the Sun Angle Analyzer
On the CD-ROM look at the movie "Pointing the Light Analyzer." This movie shows how the analyzer should be oriented with respect to the light source (step 4a. above) When pointed directly at the light source, the shadow cast by the brad is minimal. Just go to the CD Home screen and click on the item under Activity 8: *Pointing the Light Analyzer.*

---

b. Partner #2 Moves the "ground" up and down. Explain that the part of the analyzer with the grid on it represents the ground. Ignoring the protractor for the moment, have the second partner practice moving the ground up and down, while partner #1 tries to keep the analyzer aligned with the light bulb. Give students time to play with the anayzers to see how this works.

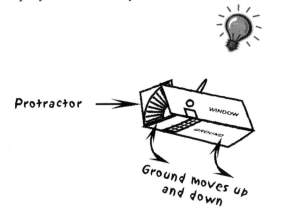

Protractor →

WINDOW

GROUND

Ground moves up and down

Note: It is important for students to understand that, in this model, the ground really does represent the ground of the Earth— changing the position of the ground represents the way the Earth's position actually does change in relation to the sunlight, due to the Earth's tilt. **That is why students should move the ground up and down, rather than the window.**

c. Try not to block the light. Both partners should try to avoid standing so that they block the light to their analyzer or someone else's. Circulate and help any students who are having trouble.

5. Regain the attention of the whole group, and ask what they have noticed. [As the ground moves up closer to the window, fewer grid squares are covered by light. Students may also notice that the light seems brighter when fewer squares are covered with light.]

6. Tell students the protractor scale is for measuring the angle of the light hitting the ground. Demonstrate how to read the angle as they push the ground up. Ask, "What angle does the protractor read when the ground is pushed all the way up to the window?" [90 degrees.] Tell them this means that the light rays are hitting the ground at 90 degrees. Another way to say that is that the light is coming down perpendicular to the ground. Show the 90 degree angle by making a T- shape with your hands.

7. Tell the students that their job is to find the angle of the light when:
   The light spreads over 4 grid squares
   The light spreads over 6 grid squares
   The light spreads over all grid squares

8. When students have finished, collect the analyzers and have them return to their seats.

Activity 8: The Angle of Sunlight

Get Out Your CD-ROM!

Using the Sun Angle Analyzer

On the CD-ROM is a movie that shows how to use the analyzer. It illustrates how the moveable side, labeled "Ground" can be rotated to demonstrate how light spreads out. As the "ground" is tilted closer to the window, the light hits more directly, as it would in summer, when the Sun appears high in the sky. As the "ground" is tilted away from the window, the light spreads out further as it would in the winter, when the Sun is lower in the sky. Just go to the CD Home screen and click on the item under Activity 8: *Using the Analyzer.*

Note: If your students are not yet at a level where they can make numerical angle measurements, skip both Step 6 and Step 7.

Students may notice that the protractor on the analyzer is different from most protractors because 0° is at the top of the arc, and 90° is at the bottom. Explain that this is done so the device will measure the angle at which sunlight is hitting the ground. Light striking perpendicular to the ground should give a 90° reading.

Discussing the Sun Angle Analyzer Results

The Sun angle of 90° happens at the equator, but at most latitudes, the Sun angle never actually gets that high. The main point to convey is that the angle of sunlight is higher in summer, lower in winter.

1. Ask for the angle of light when only four grid squares were filled with light. [90°]

2. Ask for the light angle when six grid squares were filled with light. [answers may vary] What about when all grid squares were filled? [small angle] Acknowledge that variation in answers may be due to imprecision of the instrument and inaccuracies in measurement.

3. Ask if students noticed any changes in how *bright* the light looked. Ask, "At which angle is the light most concentrated, or brightest looking on the 'ground'?" [at the highest angle: 90°] "At which angle is the light least concentrated (least bright) on the 'ground'?" [at the lower angles. At 0° light concentration vanishes!]

The Earth's atmosphere also has some effect on how concentrated the sunlight is. See "Behind The Scenes" for a note on this aspect.

4. Tell students that when the light is more concentrated, the ground gets hotter. Help them relate their discoveries with the light analyzers to the Earth's seasons. [In summer, the angle of sunlight hitting the ground is higher. The light is more concentrated, so the ground gets hotter.]

Using Pencils To Model Light Rays

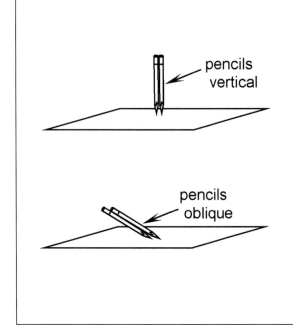

pencils vertical

pencils oblique

Another way to represent how light is less concentrated when striking the ground at a shallow angle is to use "pencils as model light rays." Take two pencils and imagine that each pencil is a bundle of millions of light rays. Hold the two pencils together and touch them to the paper so that they are perpendicular to the paper, representing the highest possible Sun angle. Wiggle the pencils so that they leave marks on the paper. Then hold the pencils so they touch the paper at a very oblique angle, sliding one pencil along the other until both tips touch the paper as shown. Wiggle the pencils again to make marks on the paper. These marks are farther apart, representing a lesser concentration of sunlight.

Seasons Unraveled

1. Remind students that the purpose of the original Seasons Survey was to find out what students (and their families) understood about the causes of seasons. Have students take the Seasons Survey again, or go over it together with them now.

2. Ask what they now think about question #3:

> **Why do you think it is hotter in the United States in June than in December? Circle all that are correct.**
>
> A. Because the Sun itself gives off more heat and light energy in June and less in December.
>
> B. Because the Earth is closer to the Sun in June, and farther away from the Sun in December.
>
> C. Because the United States is closer to the Sun in June and farther from the Sun in December.
>
> D. Because the United States is facing more toward the Sun in June and away from the Sun in December, so there are more hours of daylight in June.
>
> E. Because the Sun gets higher in the sky in June, so its rays are more concentrated on the ground.
>
> F. Because the Moon blocks out the Sun more in December.

3. Ask what answers they would pick now. [D and E]

4. Discuss the different answers, referring back to the activities students did. If they pick C, remind them that the United States *is* tilted toward the Sun in June, so it's technically a bit closer, but that doesn't change its distance from the Sun enough to make it hotter there due to the change in distance. (See the discussion in "Behind the Scenes" for more about these responses.)

5. Explain that the Earth's axis is tilted by about 23° with respect to the Earth's orbit around the Sun. The spin axes of other planets have different tilt angles. Uranus' tilt angle, for example is nearly 90°! Ask students what they think seasons might be like on Uranus. [We might predict extremely hot summers and extremely cold winters. Most regions of the planet would experience Midnight Sun for half the year and complete darkness the other half of the year!] Add that Uranus is actually a cold gas giant planet, and it is very different from Earth in many other respects as well. (The question about seasons on Uranus could also serve as a revealing assessment question.)

See the "Behind the Scenes" section for more about seasons on other planets. Both the CD-ROM and the "Resources" section in the back of this guide have web sites that detail how seasons are envisioned on other planets.

6. You may want to encourage a brief discussion about the ways that increased heat and more hours of daylight (or decreased heat and fewer hours of daylight) lead to greater or less plant growth, fit in with the life cycles of organisms, affect the weather, and have other effects that we consider part of "the seasons."

7. Ask students if they have additional questions or issues to raise about the reasons for the seasons. Some of these questions may provide a chance to re-emphasize the main ideas of the unit. Others may raise new and interesting issues. If so, discuss ways that you and the class could investigate these new questions and issues, and consider assigning individual or group projects to research and investigate these topics.

8. Conclude by pointing out that this unit, designed to help them work through the reasons for the seasons for themselves, demonstrates that the main causes of the seasonal changes we experience on Earth derive from **the relation of the Sun to the Earth.** Astronomers call this a *Sun-Earth Connection.*

If not all your students have completely grasped the reasons for the seasons, remember that overcoming misconceptions happens over time. They can keep working on it, and most probably already have fewer misconceptions than many college graduates!

9. Point out that there are many other "Sun-Earth Connections." For example, the effects of sunspots and solar flares, the phenomena of space weather, and many other subjects now being explored by scientists—including scientists who helped develop and sponsor this guide, from NASA's Sun-Earth Connection Education Forum. The CD-ROM provides links to websites that relate not only to seasons but also to other Sun-Earth Connections. Learning more about the Sun is one of the most fascinating areas of modern astronomy and the field is changing rapidly as new information is gained.

10. Praise your students for their excellent scientific work throughout the unit and the leaps they've made in understanding. Encourage them to go home and discuss what they've learned abut the real reasons for the seasons—and explain the correct survey responses—to their families and friends.

Behind the Scenes (Background for Teachers)

Note: The following information is designed for the teacher, to help respond to student questions and provide basic background. It is not intended to be read out loud to students or duplicated for them to read. It primarily focuses on the Seasons Survey, and is in no sense a full treatment of the many fascinating topics in astronomy, space science, earth science, and life science that arise in connection with the rich topic of seasons. The "Resources" section and the many web links on the CD-ROM can help you and your students pursue more background information and intriguing topics in greater depth.

The Sun-Earth Survey

1. Which of the four drawings do you think best shows the shape of Earth's orbit around the Sun? (Circle the correct letter.)

The correct answer is A. The Earth's orbit is close to circular—only *very* slightly elliptical. The Sun is not closer to the Earth in summer, as many people assume. In fact, the distance from the Earth to the Sun varies only slightly, and the shortest distance happens to be in January! (Please see the longer discussion under item 3 below for more specifics on this.) If students choose answers B, C, or D, it may indicate a belief that the seasons are caused by variations in the proximity of the Earth and Sun, a very common misconception.

The misconception that the Earth's orbit is very elliptical is fostered by many illustrations in books and posters that show the orbit in perspective, from an oblique view.

(Continued on next page)

2. Which is the best drawing to show the sizes and distances between the Earth and the Sun?

Moon

A. ◯ **Earth**   ○ Moon   (**Sun**)

B. ○ **Earth**   ○ **Moon**   (**Sun**)

C. · **Earth**   **Moon** ·   **Sun is about 11 page-widths away** ⟶

(**Circle the letter of the best drawing.**)

C. is correct, because it most accurately represents the great distance between the Earth and Sun, and the great difference in sizes of the two.

3. Why do you think it is hotter in the United States in June than in December? Circle all that are correct.

A. Because the Sun itself gives off more heat and light energy in June and less in December.

B. Because the Earth is closer to the Sun in June, and farther away from the Sun in December.

C. Because the United States is closer to the Sun in June and farther from the Sun in December.

D. Because the United States is facing more toward the Sun in June and away from the Sun in December, so there are more hours of daylight in June.

E. Because the Sun gets higher in the sky in June, so its rays are more concentrated on the ground.

F. Because the Moon blocks out the Sun more in December.

G. Because in the United States, there are more hours of daylight in June than in December.

The order of the most likely answers (B, C, D, E) has been carefully considered in relation to the sequence of the unit. **Answer A** is not correct. It speaks to the possible student misconception that the Sun, in and of itself, is the sole source of seasonal changes, regardless of its position in respect to the Earth. While there is variation in the amount of heat and light energy of the Sun, there is absolutely no correlation between this variation and the months of the year or the seasons! **Answer F** is also incorrect, bringing in another factor (the Moon) and an entirely unrelated eclipse-like idea about the Moon "blocking out" the Sun in December. Again, this is not the case, and like answer A, answer F does not factor in the crucial nature of the relation between the Sun and Earth.

The most obvious and common misconception is that **Answer B** is correct. This should be cleared up in Activity 5 on the shape of the Earth's orbit. That activity demonstrates that the orbit of the Earth is very nearly circular, so that the Earth as a whole is not significantly farther away from or closer to the Sun at any time during its orbit. Interestingly enough, the Earth is closest to the Sun on January 2nd and farthest on July 4th. The Earth is about 1.5% closer to the Sun when it is winter in the Northern Hemisphere and about 1.5% farther from the Sun when it is summer in the Northern Hemisphere!

A more subtle misconception would be indicated by a student responding that **Answer C** is correct. This could indicate that the student knows that the Earth is tilted on its axis, and that—for that reason—the United States is closer to the Sun in June, even though the Sun is not closer to the Earth as a whole at that time. Answer C as a statement is technically true, but it is an incorrect survey answer because the distance "closer" to the Sun represented by the tilt is insignificant as an explanation for why it is hotter (which is what the question is asking). The student is still focusing on **distance** as the primary cause and is not aware of the key issue of scale. The student does not realize that the vast distance between the Sun and the Earth makes the tilt of the Earth irrelevant with regard to the distance between various places on Earth and the Sun. Even the whole diameter of Earth (about 12,000 kilometers) is an insignificant distance when compared with the distance from Earth to Sun (about 150,000,000 kilometers), so a distance less than the whole diameter (such as that caused by the tilt) is even less significant. As noted above, the actual Earth-Sun distance varies by about 1.5%, or from 147,000,000 to 151,000,000, and even that difference of about 4 million kilometers is not significant when compared to the overall distance.

That leaves **Answers D, E,** and **G,** all of which are correct. As the activities in the unit demonstrate, there are two main factors responsible for Earth's seasons.

Both are related to the tilt of the Earth's axis, **but neither are related to changes in distance.** The two factors are the following:

a. **More daylight hours.** The tilt of the Earth means that portions of the Earth where there is summer are facing more toward the Sun, making for more hours of daylight. Because the United States is facing more toward the Sun in June and away from the Sun in December, there are more hours of daylight in June.

b. **Angle and Concentration of Light.** At the same time, during summer the Sun's position in the sky is higher, increasing the angle of incidence of the sunlight. As the students' Sun Angle Analyzer modeled, this increases the concentration of the light on the ground, so the ground gets warmer.

It is very likely that this unit will introduce students to new ways of looking at familiar phenomena they previously did not fully understand. These are not simple ideas—it takes time to master their complexity! It is very likely that some students will continue to cling to mistaken ideas, or will combine some aspects of correct and incorrect ideas to advance their understanding but not yet achieve full comprehension. For some students, the recognition that the seasons have to do with the tilt of the Earth can be an important first step—especially if they then can take the next step to comprehend clearly that the difference in distance reflected by the tilt does not play a significant role. At the next level of understanding, and even though the unit has attempted to build and interweave these ideas carefully, it is possible that some students may more clearly understand only one of the two main causative factors (for example, why there are more hours of daylight) and not the other (the angle of incidence and concentration of light)—or vice versa. Both require a fairly sophisticated visualization of the relative and always-changing positions of the Earth and the Sun. Students will have reached the highest level of understanding when they are able to take into account (and explain in their own words) the impact of both of these factors. Advanced students will recognize that there is a complex interplay between these two factors which in turn gives rise to conditions that introduce the many changes in plant growth, life cycles, weather, and other characteristics that we attribute to "the seasons."

What about the effect of the Earth's atmosphere?

Yet another factor related to the Sun's angle and the concentration of light has to do with how much atmosphere the sunlight has to pass through before striking the ground. Light scatters as it goes through the air, so at low Sun angles (point B) light is less concentrated, not only because it spreads out more, but also because less of it reaches the ground. However, this effect is minor compared with the other causes of seasons already discussed.

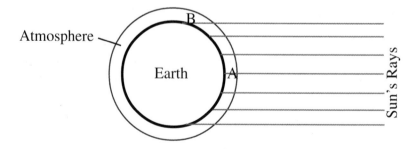

You or your students might encounter the question: If we say the Earth's axis is tilted—tilted with respect to what? Any tilt of Earth's axis is with reference to Earth's orbit around the Sun. Earth's orbit defines a plane in space, known as the ***plane of the ecliptic.*** The word *ecliptic* actually means the apparent path that the Sun *appears to* travel through the sky as the Earth moves around the Sun.

Some Interesting, Instructive, and Amusing E-Mails on Seasons

How Many Seasons Are There Near the Equator?

Date: Fri, 12 Feb 1999
One more perspective on the seasons—when I served in the Peace Corps in south India, I learned that the concept of four seasons was unknown in at least that tropical part of the world. There were three seasons, the hot season, the rainy or monsoon season, and the cold season. These were unrelated to the equinoxes and the solstices. If memory serves me correctly, the rainy season seemed to start shortly after the zenith passage of the Sun, although there was no general mention of the Sun's position (probably since the Sun was near the zenith for much of the year). The season "officially" started with the first monsoon rain, or when the monsoon clouds had moved that far north.
—Sheldon Schafer, Director of Science Programs and Facilities
Lakeview Museum of Arts & Sciences
http://www.lakeview-museum.org
Home of the World's Largest Model of the Solar System
http://www.bradley.edu/las/phy/solar_system.html

Date: Sun, 14 Feb 1999
Here in Phoenix, we're not really close to the Equator, but they still joke about our two seasons: Summer and Not-Summer. They call the rains in July and August "monsoon season" but it is hardly comparable to a true monsoon.
—Christine Shupla, Planetarium Manager, Arizona Science Center

Date: Sun, 14 Feb 99
I grew up in La Paz, Bolivia, located around 15 degrees South (I think) at close to 12,000 ft altitude. There are two seasons: the dry season and the rainy season. For most people in the area, this is really what matters, regardless of the Sun's wanderings.

Incidentally, a little joke: the Spanish word for "season" is "estacion," which also happens to be the word for "station." Since it is usually relatively cold in La Paz, people joke that there are two seasons: the winter season and the train station...
—Andres Dandler (Dartmouth)

Date: Sun, 14 Feb 1999
...in Illinois we only have two seasons — winter and road repair. Road repair solstice — April 1. Winter solstice — December 1.
—Jeffrey L. Hunt, Ed.D., Director of Instructional Technology
Indian Prairie School District 204, Naperville, Illinois

Date: Mon, 15 Feb 1999
We in South Florida have only two seasons: warm, and warmer.
— David Menke, Buehler Planetarium, Ft. Lauderdale

Asteroids Have Seasons, Too

We don't often think of asteroids as having seasons, but they do. Like Earth, the asteroid named Eros passes through two solstices (when the Sun shines down over the poles) and two equinoxes (when day and night are of equal length) during its 1.76 year circuit around the Sun. The names of the seasons on Eros are the same as the ones on Earth — fall, winter, summer, and spring — but that's where the similarities end. Seasons on Eros last different lengths of time (northern spring is only half as long as autumn) while the apparent size of the Sun nearly doubles between fall and spring. The difference in polar surface temperatures from summer to winter may be as great as the difference between liquid nitrogen and boiling water. Seasons on Eros are truly "alien"

As your students discover in the unit. Earth's seasons are caused by the 23.5° tilt of our planet's axis. The orbit of Eros, on the other hand, is highly elliptical and its spin axis is tilted 89 degrees! Eros's elliptical orbit affects the length of its seasons because the asteroid travels faster when its closer to the Sun than it does when it's farther away. For this reason northern spring on Eros is three and a half Earth-months long (about the same as the length of springtime on our planet) while autumn persists for seven Earth-months. These values are reversed in the asteroid's southern hemisphere.

Interplanetary Seasons

Extraterrestrial seasons are hardly noticeable on some planets (Venus), mindbogglingly extreme on others (Uranus) and in some cases simply impossible to define (Mercury). Planetary seasons are caused by two factors: axial tilt and variable distance from the Sun (orbital eccentricity). As this unit helps students to understand, Earth's orbit is nearly circular and so has little effect on climate. It is the axial tilt that causes almost all seasonal changes.

Jupiter and Venus have very small axial tilts—just 3°. Seasonal changes on those planets are correspondingly small. Spring on Venus isn't much different from autumn there. The planet's dense, acidic atmosphere produces a runaway greenhouse effect that keeps the surface at 750 K year-round — that's hot enough to melt lead. Spring fever on Venus is really hot!

Mars, on the other hand, has the highest orbital eccentricity of any planet except Pluto. Its distance from the Sun varies between 1.64 and 1.36 AU (astronomical units) over the Martian year. This large variation, combined with an axial tilt greater than Earth's, gives rise to seasonal changes far greater than we experience even in Antarctica.

Note: The information on pages 94 and 95 is modified and adapted from educational articles found at Science@NASA Home.

From the point of view of an Earth-dweller, one of the strangest effects of seasons on Mars is the change in atmospheric pressure. During winter the global atmospheric pressure on Mars is 25% lower than during summer. This happens because of the eccentricity of Mars's orbit and a complex exchange of carbon dioxide between Mars's dry-ice polar caps and its CO2 atmosphere. Around the summer solstice when the Martian north pole is tilted away from the sun, the northern polar cap expands as carbon dioxide in the polar atmosphere freezes. At the other end of the planet the southern polar cap melts, giving CO2 back to the atmosphere. This process reverses half a year later at the winter solstice.

At first it might seem that these events occurring at opposite ends of Mars would simply balance out over the course of the Martian year, having no net effect on climate. But they don't. That's because Mars is 10% closer to the Sun in winter than it is in summer. At the time of the winter solstice the northern polar cap absorbs more CO2 than the southern polar cap absorbs half a year later. The difference is so great that Mars's atmosphere is noticeably thinner during winter.

Martian seasons are peculiar by Earth standards, but they probably pale in comparison to seasons on Uranus. Like Earth, the orbit of Uranus is nearly circular so it keeps the same distance from the Sun throughout its long year. But, Uranus's spin axis is tilted by a whopping 82°! This gives rise to extreme 20-year-long seasons and unusual weather. For nearly a quarter of the Uranian year (equal to 84 Earth years), the Sun shines directly over each pole, leaving the other half of the planet plunged into a long, dark, cold winter.

The Northern Hemisphere of Uranus is just now emerging from this winter. As the sunlight reaches some latitudes for the first time in years, it warms the atmosphere and triggers gigantic springtime storms comparable in size to North America with temperatures of 300 degrees below zero. On the next page, we reprint a NASA press release noting the first-ever view of one such storm.

Mercury's seasons — if they can be called that — are very confusing. Until the 1960s it was thought that Mercury's "day" was the same length as its "year" keeping the same face to the Sun much as the Moon does to the Earth. This was shown to be incorrect by Doppler radar observations. We now know that Mercury rotates three times during two of its years. Mercury is the only body in the solar system tidally locked into an orbital-to-rotational resonance with a ratio other than 1:1. This fact and the high eccentricity of Mercury's orbit are thought likely to produce very strange effects for an observer on Mercury's surface, including changes in the apparent size of the Sun and perceived reverses in the Sun's path through the Mercurial sky!. Temperature variations on Mercury are the most extreme in the solar system, ranging from 90 K at night to 700 K during the day.

HUGE SPRING STORMS ROUSE URANUS FROM WINTER HIBERNATION

If springtime on Earth were anything like it will be on Uranus, we would be experiencing waves of massive storms, each one covering the country from Kansas to New York, with temperatures of 300 degrees below zero.

A dramatic new time-lapse movie by NASA's Hubble Space Telescope shows for the first time seasonal changes on the planet. Once considered one of the blander-looking planets, Uranus is now revealed as a dynamic world with the brightest clouds in the outer Solar System and a fragile ring system that wobbles like an unbalanced wagon wheel. The clouds are probably made of crystals of methane, which condense as warm bubbles of gas well up from deep in the atmosphere of Uranus.

The movie, created by Hubble researcher Erich Karkoschka of the University of Arizona, clearly shows for the first time the wobble in the ring system, which is made of billions of tiny pebbles. This wobble may be caused by Uranus' shape, which is like a slightly flattened globe, along with the gravitational tug from its many moons.

Although Uranus has been observed for more than 200 years, "no one has ever seen this view in the modern era of astronomy because of the long year of Uranus — more than 84 Earth years," said Dr. Heidi Hammel, Massachusetts Institute of Technology.

The seasonal changes on Earth are caused by our planet's rotational pole being slightly tilted. Consequently, the Earth's Southern and Northern hemispheres are alternately tipped toward or away from the Sun as the Earth moves around its orbit. Uranus is tilted completely over on its side, giving rise to extreme 20- year-long seasons and unusual weather. For nearly a quarter of the Uranian year, the sun shines directly over each pole, leaving the other half of the planet plunged into a long, dark, frigid winter.

The Northern Hemisphere of Uranus is just now coming out of the grip of its decades-long winter. As the sunlight reaches some latitudes, it warms the atmosphere. This appears to be causing the atmosphere to come out of a frigid hibernation and stir back to life. Uranus does not have a solid surface, but is instead a ball of mostly hydrogen and helium. Absorption of red light by methane in the atmosphere gives the planet its cyan color.

Uranus was discovered March 13, 1781, by William Herschel. Early visual observers reported Jupiter-like cloud belts on the planet, but when NASA's Voyager 2 flew by in 1986, Uranus appeared as featureless as a cue ball. In the past 13 years, the planet has moved far enough along its orbit for the sun to shine at mid-latitudes in the Northern Hemisphere. By the year 2007, the sun will be shining directly over Uranus' equator.

Karkoschka, Hammel and other investigators used Hubble from 1994 through 1998 to take images of Uranus in both visible and near-infrared light.

The Space Telescope Science Institute is operated by the Association of Universities for Research in Astronomy, Inc. for NASA, under contract with NASA's Goddard Space Flight Center, Greenbelt, MD. The Hubble Space Telescope is a project of international cooperation between NASA and the European Space Agency.

http://oposite.stsci.edu/pubinfo/latest.html http://oposite.stsci.edu/pubinfo/pictures.html

Of Seasons and Sunflowers

Date: Sun, 7 Sep 1997 10:43:44 -0400 (EDT)
From: David Linton
To: Planetarian's Digest
Subject: Sunflower Story-Reply to Floral Fiesta

The responses by Tom Hocking and Kevin Conod to a question by Dennis Mamana referred to a sunflower being used as a kind of "suntracker." I like the idea. In some planetarium, years ago, I picked up an idea to use a sunflower in describing how the Sun travels across the sky as seen from the North Pole (South Pole works too!). I still regularly use this story in my introductory college classes. High schoolers love it, too. I believe it serves to cement in place an understanding of the solar motion I have just demonstrated to them. The story goes something like this:

Hearing that there were six consecutive months of 24-hour daylight at the North Pole, a professor of agriculture at (insert the name of your least favorite University) suggested that the North Pole would be a great place to grow sunflowers. [Pause] Yes, he knew that it's cold there, so the experiment was done in a heated greenhouse in northern Canada or Alaska. And the experiment worked fine — for awhile! The sunflowers sprouted, grew taller, and blossomed. And then, shortly thereafter, they all died. Can you tell me why? [No one has ever offered the "correct" answer] Well, look over here [as I turn up my console lights, and simulate a sunflower with my hand, the stem with my forearm, and the roots with my elbow]. The sunflowers had their roots firmly stuck in the soil, and they followed the Sun — sunflowers are said to be "phototropic". Where we are, in Illinois, the flowers have a chance to reset themselves overnight (just as some of you may choose to "unwind" at the end of the day), but the sunflowers don't get a chance to do this at the North Pole—the Sun just goes around and around in a circle. After a few days, the poor sunflowers had all strangled themselves. [I follow this story with a statement that even if the story isn't true, it ought to be; and that "I hope that this story helps each of you to remember how the Sun (and the stars, too) move in the polar sky."]

Recounting this story here also causes me to suggest (to Dennis) that you might develop some displays or a show for your Floral Fiesta which uses as a theme the "greenhouse effect"—it's certainly important for flowers (and all us other living things).

David Linton
Professor of Astronomy
Parkland College
Champaign, IL

Summer Vacations in the Southern Hemisphere.

Date: 12 Jan 99

Answers to questions about summer vacations in the Southern Hemisphere.

1. Do or did people in the Southern Hemisphere celebrate either the summer or winter solstice?

Yes, for sure. When the Incas were around (before the Spanish Colony dominated them in the 16th century) they worshiped the Sun, their main god. In temples everywhere still found today, you can see ceremonial stones, with some of the sides pointing directly to the spot on the horizon where sunrise occurs during a solstice (either winter or summer, depending on the temple). They carried out ceremonies at those times.

More recently, in '92 I went to Tiahuanacu, a pre-Inca site near Lake Titicaca, where the local population still carries out a traditional ceremony at sunrise on June 21, the winter solstice. The colorful ceremony includes some offerings, dances, etc., asking the Sun to return South again. It works!

As the Spanish Conquest imposed Catholic religion on the local population, an interesting blend has occurred, where people are Catholic, but still give offerings to the pre-conquest gods, especially the Sun and "Pachamama," Mother Earth. You have to wonder whether Catholicism was absorbed into the local traditions or whether the local traditions were absorbed into Catholicism. But that's a different story.

2. If schools only operate for 10 months out of the year, are they currently on summer break in January?

Correct. Some foreign schools (especially the American School) operate on a northern schedule, so that people moving back and forth between the US and that country will not lose (or gain) half a year every time they move. As you can imagine, this leads to major problems when people from that country switch in or out of that school. There is no perfect solution.

I went to a German School, but it followed the southern calendar. However, the German teachers and administrators always pushed for longer vacations in July-August, so that their kids could go back to Germany for the summer. But the local teachers and administrators pushed for longer vacations during the southern summer. They had to reach some compromise.

—Andres Dandler (grew up in Bolivia and Peru)

For the "Going Further" Activity after Activity 6: Seasonal Changes in Sun Position (see page 70)

First show the "Single Day Sun Movement" chart overhead transparency (master for photocopy on page 104) and point out where the Sun rises in the east, sets in the west, and reaches a peak "elevation angle" at about noon each day. Make sure the class understands that the "degrees" used here are **not** temperature degrees, but the same kind of degree the class used to measure latitude and longitude: i.e. degrees related to a 360° full circle.

Define the terms azimuth angle (angle measured horizontally along the horizon) and elevation angle (angle measured vertically upwards from the horizon). The zenith is the "highest" place in the sky, at 90° elevation angle. Elevation angle is also known as "altitude angle." Caution students about being careful not to misinterpret these words. Elevation or altitude means "height above the ground"— unless it is followed by the word "angle." The meanings and units are different. Elevation is measured in units of length, such as meters, but the elevation angle is measured in degrees.

See the instructions for this "Going Further" on page 70 of this guide. If you decide to try it, the data sheets and other information for duplication can be found on the next five pages (page 100–104).

Strengthening Understanding of World Coordinate System: Latitude and Longitude

If your students need better understanding of and proficiency with finding things on Earth by latitude and longitude, spend some extra time having them practice locating places on Earth specifying coordinates, latitude and longitude. There are many ways to do this. Here are two:

a. Have each student choose a particular continent, write down the coordinates (latitude and longitude) of someplace within that continent, and then challenge a partner to determine what continent is, given only the coordinates and a world map. This could also be done with countries or cities.

b. Coordinate Game: call out the coordinates of a particular city and have students find what city it is. First student to find the correct city gets to choose and call out the coordinates of the next city.

> **Data Sheets and Related Information for the "Going Further" activity on Seasonal Changes in Sun Position are on the next five pages (100-104).**

Seasonal Changes in Sun Position

Data for each month On the 21st day of the month-; generated with Voyager by Carina software, Hayward, California

Latitude: 70 degrees North

Date	Sunrise Azimuth	Noon Altitude	Sunset Azimuth
Jan	—	0°	—
Feb	-35°	8°	-35°
Mar	0°	20°	0°
Apr	35°	30°	35°
May	—	40° S	—
Jun	—	43° S	—
Jul	—	40° S	—
Aug	35°	30°	35°
Sep	0°	20°	0°
Oct	-35°	8°	-35°
Nov	—	0°	—
Dec	—	not up	—

Troms□, NORWAY Prudhoe Bay, ALASKA, USA; Clyde, Baffin Island, CANADA

Latitude: 57 degrees North

Date	Sunrise Azimuth	Noon Altitude	Sunset Azimuth
Jan	-37°	13° S	-37°
Feb	-18°	23° S	-18°
Mar	0°	33° S	0°
Apr	22°	44° S	22°
May	40°	53° S	40°
Jun	49°	56° S	49°
Jul	41°	53° S	41°
Aug	24°	45° S	23°
Sep	0°	33° S	0°
Oct	-19°	22° S	-19°
Nov	-37°	13° S	-37°
Dec	-45°	9° S	-45°

Kodiak, ALASKA, USA; Glasgow, SCOTLAND; Copenhagen, DENMARK Moscow, RUSSIA

Latitude: 38 degrees North

Date	Sunrise Azimuth	Noon Altitude	Sunset Azimuth
Jan	-26°	32° S	-26°
Feb	-13°	42° S	-13°
Mar	0°	52° S	0°
Apr	16°	64° S	16°
May	26°	72° S	26°
Jun	31°	75° S	31°
Jul	26°	72° S	26°
Aug	16°	64° S	16°
Sep	0°	52° S	0°
Oct	-13°	41° S	-13°
Nov	-26°	32° S	-26°
Dec	-31°	28° S	-31°

USA: San Francisco, CALIFORNIA; Charleston, W. VIRGINIA; Wichita, KANSAS St. Louis, MISSOURI; Louisville, KENTUCKY;   Pueblo, COLORADO; Richmond, VIRGINIA
Sendai, JAPAN   Seoul, S. KOREA
Tientsin, CHINA   Izmir, TURKEY
Athens, GREECE   Palermo, SICILY
Cordoba, SPAIN   Lisbon, PORTUGAL

Latitude: 26 degrees North

Date	Sunrise Azimuth	Noon Altitude	Sunset Azimuth
Jan	-22°	44° S	-22°
Feb	-11°	53° S	-11°
Mar	0°	65° S	0°
Apr	14°	76° S	14°
May	23°	84° S	23°
Jun	27°	87° S	27°
Jul	23°	84° S	23°
Aug	14°	76° S	14°
Sep	0	65° S	0
Oct	-11°	53° S	-11°
Nov	-22°	44° S	-22°
Dec	-27°	41° S	-27°

Monterey, MEXICO Taipei, TAIWAN
Kunming CHINA   Patna, INDIA Karachi,
PAKISTAN   Riyadh, SAUDI ARABIA
Luxor, EGYPT   Wau El Kebir, LIBYA

Latitude: 0 degrees

Date	Sunrise Azimuth	Noon Altitude	Sunset Azimuth
Jan	-20°	70° S	-20°
Feb	-10°	79° S	-10°
Mar	0°	90°	0°
Apr	12°	78° N	12°
May	20°	70° N	20°
Jun	24°	66° N	23°
Jul	20°	69° N	20°
Aug	12°	78° N	12°
Sep	0°	90°	0°
Oct	-11°	79° S	-11°
Nov	-20°	70° S	-20°
Dec	-23°	66° S	-23°

Quito, ECUADOR; Nairobi, KENYA; Singapore, MALAYA

Latitude: 26 degrees South

Date	Sunrise Azimuth	Noon Altitude	Sunset Azimuth
Jan	-22°	84° N	-22°
Feb	-11°	76° N	-11°
Mar	0°	65° N	0°
Apr	14°	53° N	14°
May	23°	44° N	23°
Jun	27°	41° N	27°
Jul	23°	44° N	23°
Aug	14°	53° N	14°
Sep	0	65° N	0
Oct	-11°	76° N	-11°
Nov	-22°	84° N	-22°
Dec	-27°	87° S	-27°

Pretoria, SOUTH AFRICA; Curitiba, BRAZIL Brisbane, AUSTRALIA; Asuncion, PARAGUAY

Latitude: 38 degrees South

Date	Sunrise Azimuth	Noon Altitude	Sunset Azimuth
Jan	-26°	72° N	-26°
Feb	-13°	62° N	-13°
Mar	0°	52° N	0°
Apr	16°	40° N	16°
May	26°	32° N	26°
Jun	31°	29° N	31°
Jul	26°	32° N	26°
Aug	16°	40° N	16°
Sep	0°	52° N	0°
Oct	-13°	63° N	-13°
Nov	-26°	72° N	-26°
Dec	-31°	75° N	-31°

Melbourne, AUSTRALIA; Auckland, NEW ZEALAND; Bahia Blanca, ARGENTINA Curacautin, CHILE

Latitude: 70 degrees South

Date	Sunrise Azimuth	Noon Altitude	Sunset Azimuth
Jan	—	40° N	—
Feb	-35°	30° N	-35°
Mar	0°	20° N	0°
Apr	35°	8° N	35°
May	—	0° N	—
Jun	—	Not up	—
Jul	—	0° N	—
Aug	35°	8° N	35°
Sep	0°	20° N	0°
Oct	-35°	30° N	-35°
Nov	—	40° N	—
Dec	—	43° N	—

ANTARCTICA

Name: _____

Sunset Positions

Use the data in the "Seasonal Changes in Sun Position" tables to plot on this chart where on the horizon the Sun rises and sets each month—how many degrees north or south of due West. If you plot for more than one latitude, use a color code to distinguish them.

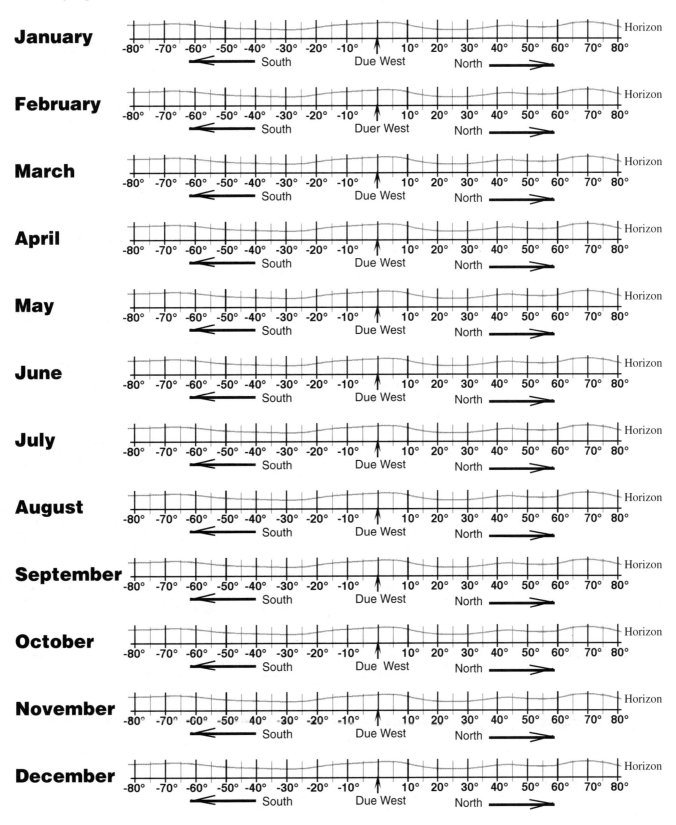

Name: _____

Sunrise Positions

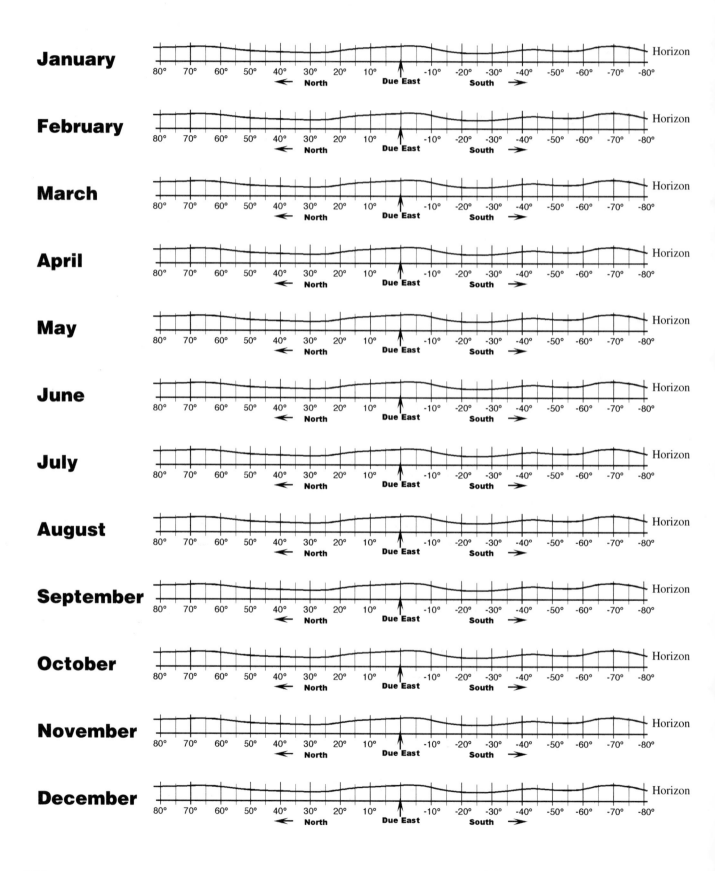

LHS GEMS: *The Real Reasons for Seasons*

Name: _____

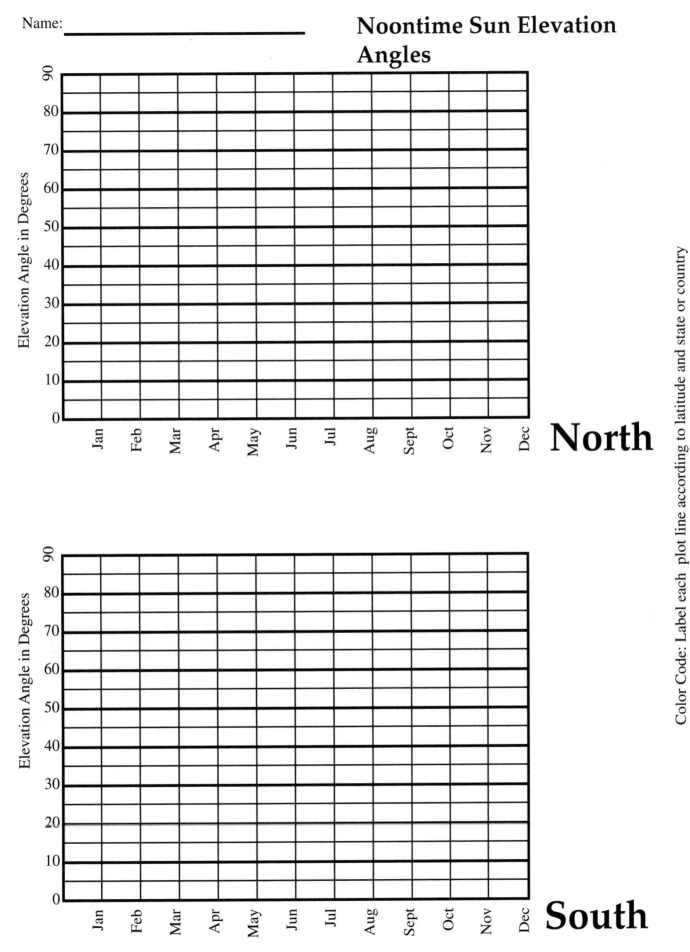

North

Elevation Angle in Degrees

Jan Feb Mar Apr May Jun Jul Aug Sept Oct Nov Dec

South

Elevation Angle in Degrees

Jan Feb Mar Apr May Jun Jul Aug Sept Oct Nov Dec

Color Code: Label each plot line according to latitude and state or country

Behind the Scenes

Single Day Sun Movement

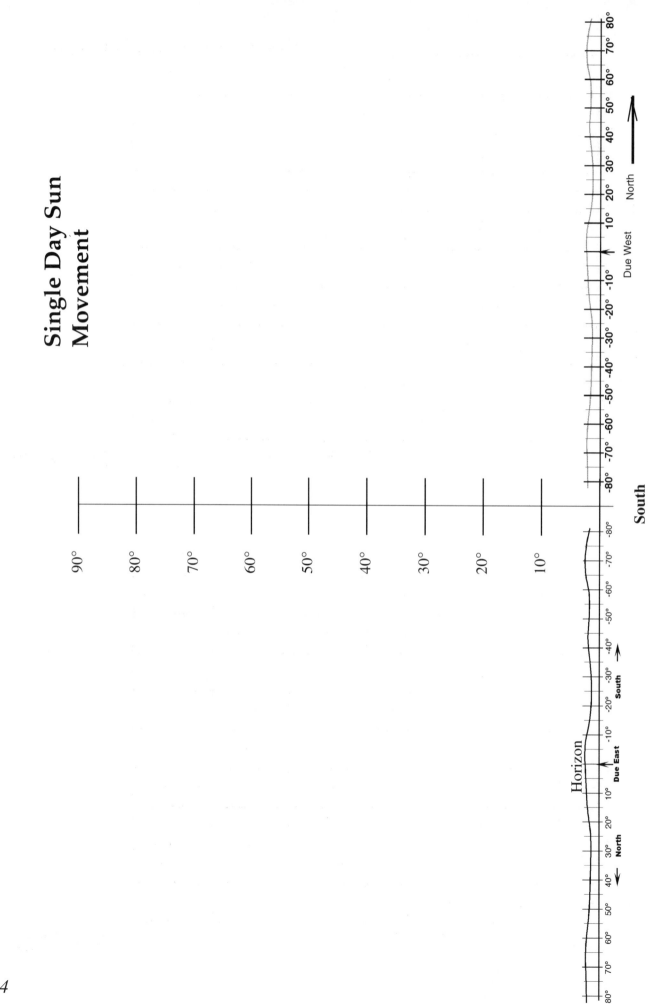

Assessment Suggestions

Selected Student Outcomes

1. Students are able to systematically work through any mistaken ideas they may have had to develop a more accurate scientific understanding of the reasons for seasons.

2, Students can articulate how the connection between the Earth and the Sun creates seasons—taking into account Earth's revolution around the Sun, the 23° tilt of the Earth's axis, the impact of this tilt on the number of hours of daylight at different times of the year, and the effect of the angle of incidence of the Sun's light as it strikes the Earth.

3. Students are able to explain why the most common misconceptions about the reasons for the seasons are not accurate, especially the idea that seasons are directly related to and caused by changing distances between the Earth and Sun.

4. Students demonstrate an increased understanding of, and ability to explain and apply, astronomical concepts and models, including the spherical shape of the Earth and Sun, planetary orbits and axis rotation, ellipses, and the scale of the solar system.

Built-In Assessment Activities

The Seasons Survey and Recurrent Discussions. In Activity 2, students fill out the Sun-Earth Survey for the first time, before surveying friends and family. Their initial responses to the survey provide a baseline to assist you in assessing what they know about the reasons for the seasons and related topics.   During the subsequent sessions in the unit, the class returns to specific questions and re-evaluates their responses in light of what they have learned in that activity. Probing questions are suggested throughout so students will explain their reasoning. These discussions can provide the teacher with a sense of how students are progressing in their understanding. In the last activity, students take the seasons survey again (or the entire class goes through it).   If they each fill out the survey again, their responses can be compared to their initial ones. If it is an all-class discussion, the teacher can observe those who display the most cogent reasoning.   In a sense, the entire guide is a logical progression of activities designed to help students—not simply circle correct answers—but understand in-depth the reasoning and scientific basis for them. See the "Behind the Scenes" section for more detailed information on the reasoning involved in the correct survey responses. Teachers may also want to have students write a letter or essay on the reasons for the seasons or in some other way communicate their reasoning in writing. (Outcomes 1, 2, 3, 4)

(Continued on next page)

Assessment Suggestions *(continued)*

Scale Model and Ellipse. In Activities 3 and 4 students take a trip to the Sun, make a scale model, and investigate ellipses. Their understanding of the vast distance between the Earth and Sun is important to their ability to understand that relatively small changes in distance have little impact when compared to the entire distance. In the eclipse drawing activity, students learn that, contrary to many depictions, the Earth's orbit around the Sun is very nearly circular, which helps them see that the orbit does not affect distance in a significant way. In the discussion that follows the ellipse activity, and in the discussions in later sessions, the teacher can be alert for student comments and explanations that demonstrate, or fail to demonstrate, this understanding. (Outcomes 3, 4)

Graphing Temperatures and Length of Daylight Hours. In these activities, students graph temperature data and discover the reversal pattern of seasons in the Northern and Southern hemispheres and that day lengths in the two hemispheres are mirror images of each other. Student graphs, discussion, questions they ask, and problems they encounter can provide information to the teacher on how well students grasp these ideas, and how well they are able to integrate these understandings with the earlier sessions and lessons of the unit. (Outcomes 1, 2)

The Tilt's the Thing. In Activity 7, students first model the distribution of light during rotation of a non-tilted Earth, then a tilted one, and see how the tilt causes differences in the duration of day and night in different hemispheres. The ensuing discussion can help teachers gauge progress in understanding, especially during the re-discussion of scale. Now that the tilt has been modeled, some students may inadvertently raise the rather persistent but mistaken idea that the difference in distance from the Sun caused by the tilt is significant enough to impact seasons. (Outcomes 1, 2, 3)

Analyzing the Angle and Summing Up. In Activity 8, students use a sun angle analyzer to consider the effect of the Sun's apparent height in the sky and learn that when the light is more concentrated, the ground gets hotter. This discussion and the summing up session that follows can assist the teacher in seeing how full a grasp of the reasons for the seasons students have, and if there are gaps in understanding and/or other issues and questions that may call for additional activities and discussions. While some students may be able to acquire a full understanding, many of the ideas and visualizations involved are complex. It is important for the middle school teacher to understand that there will be a continuum of understanding. Experiencing this unit by itself may not bring all students to a sophisticated level, but if progress on key conceptual benchmarks along the way can be seen, that should be recognized as a positive achievement. (Outcomes 1, 2, 4)

Additional Assessment Activities

Seasons on Uranus. At the end of the unit, students are asked how a different tilt of spin axis might affect seasons on other planets, in particular Uranus, which has a tilt angle of nearly 90°! You could make this a writing assignment, or a topic for a group presentation. In visualizing seasons on this planet, students should not only describe the seasons they predict, but explain the reasons for those seasons. Extra credit could be given to students or groups who do additional research about the planet, so the other characteristics that make it markedly different from Earth are considered. (Outcome 2)

Linking the Sun-Earth Connection to Other Seasonal Attributes. In a brief discussion, students are asked to consider how the basic elements of the seasons they've investigated in the unit (heat or cold, more or less daylight, angle of sunlight) are linked to plant growth, life cycles of organisms, weather, rituals, and holidays generally associated with seasons. Students could be asked to write an essay or make a detailed flowchart on this subject, with emphasis on how well they are able to describe and elaborate these connections. (Outcome 2)

Cross-Hemispheric Writing Assignment. Have students write a letter to an imaginary friend in the Southern Hemisphere describing in detail the season that is happening where the letter writer lives and explaining why and how they know that the season where the friend lives is quite different. The letter could refer directly to experiences and information students gained in the unit. (If you're teaching this in the Southern Hemisphere then reverse the assignment!) (Outcomes 2, 3)

Letter to a Fourth-Grader. Suppose that a fourth grade class was asked what causes the seasons, and all of them said that when the Sun was closer to the Earth, it was spring and summer, and when the Sun was farther away, it was fall and winter. Students could be assigned to explain, in a letter to a fourth grader, in as accessible a way as possible, why this is not the case. They will probably want to include some drawings. (Outcomes 2, 4)

Special Note: The Seasons CD-ROM packaged with this guide includes a trial version of the Seasons software program from Riverside Scientific that allows students to model what happens when key variables are changed, such as the Earth's tilt and the shape of the Earth's orbit. Also on the CD is Starry Night, a desktop planetarium program from Sienna Software (Space.Com) that allows students to explore and manipulate many displays and movements of the solar system and beyond. Either or both of these programs could be utilized by individual students or student groups to demonstrate their thinking about seasons to the class, or could be used in other assessments of your own devising. We welcome your ideas!

Resources

There are many resources provided directly on the CD-ROM that accompanies this GEMS unit. The list below includes some of the most useful of these, as well as several resource books. While we have listed some web addresses below, please note that these are subject to change. On the CD we have "addressed" that issue by linking you first to the Lawrence Hall of Science and then to the site—in this way we can keep the links updated and spare you the time and trouble of finding a new address!

Resource Books/Guides

Earth Moon, and Stars. This classic GEMS guide by Cary Sneider, who was kind enough to review this GEMS guide, remains one of the best ways to present important basic astronomy concepts, including the spherical nature of the Earth and gravity, with activities as well on moon phases and star clocks. For more on this and other astronomy and space science GEMS guides, such as *Moons of Jupiter* and *Messages from Space*, go to: lawrencehallofscience.org/gems/

The Astronomy Cafe: 365 questions and answers from Ask the Astronomer by Sten Odenwald, W.H. Freeman and Company, 1998. This book answers 365 popular questions about astronomy, many of them having to do with the sun and planets. The author has a new book *entitled The 23rd Cycle: Learning to live with a stormy star* due out in December 2000 and hosts a great web site. (See listing for Astronomy Café below.) Dr. Odenwald also served as a scientific reviewer for this GEMS guide.

The Reasons for Seasons: The Great Cosmic Megagalactic Trip Without Moving from Your Chair by Linda Allison, Brown Paper School series, Little Brown, 1998. This wonderfully subtitled book has many activities, including some aimed at helping students understand seasons as a result of the relation of the Earth to the Sun. Currently listed as out of print, it may well be in many school or public libraries.

Learning About the Changing Seasons (Little Scientists: A Hand-On Approach to Learning series) by Heidi Gold-Dworkin, Donna Goodman Lee, Robert K. Ullman, McGraw-Hill, 2000. Although designed to appeal to younger students, the concepts explored could make a nice connection to the guide, including a section on the "reasons for the seasons." It includes hands-on experiments, a glossary, and reading list. The lead author is a Nobel Prize-winning biochemist who heads the "Little Scientist" series.

Onto the World Wide Web

As the introduction to this guide describes, the **Private Universe** project has done important work on student misconceptions, including those concerning the seasons. A videotape and many other resources are available from the Private Universe: Teacher's Lab, Annenberg/CPB Math and Science Project, at:
http://www.learner.org/teacherslab/pup/index.html

Developed by NASA's Office of Space Science, the **Space Science Education Resource Directory** provides easy access to a wealth of electronic resources (web site and downloadable files) to help you teach important space science concepts. This site serves as your gateway to NASA's space science resources for educators!
http://teachspacescience.stsci.edu

Brought to you by the same people who helped GEMS bring you this guide, we very highly recommend **Science Education Gateway (SEGway)** as a great place to get free curriculum material developed for K–12 on a variety of astronomy subjects. Also sponsored by NASA's Office of Space Science, the SEGWAY project is hosted by the Center for Science Education at Space Sciences Laboratory, University of California, Berkeley. http://cse.ssl.berkeley.edu/SEGway/

Your students may also find it interesting to be a weather reporter on Mars, and to compare seasons on Earth and Mars. The *Martian Sun Times* lesson can be found through the SEGway website or at: http://www.ucls.uchicago.edu/MartianSunTimes/index.html

Speaking of NASA, which has great wealth of resources, here are additional helpful links:

NASA SpaceLink. The starting point and good way to tap into NASA's extensive resources for educators.
http://spacelink.nasa.gov/

A good NASA listing specifically for educators, featuring ways to contact the regional NASA education resource center network all around the country, can be found at:
http://soho.nascom.nasa.gov/explore/NASA_Ed_Resources.html

And still more:

Thursday's Classroom. The aim of Thursday's Classroom is to provide a lasting connection between NASA's latest research and the classroom environment. It includes many well-thought-out lesson plans and resources on a diverse range of topics. An archive allows you to access past lessons. The September 22, 2000 edition, as just one of many examples, has a number of connections to the topic of seasons. Several GEMS activities have been adapted on this web site.
http://www.thursdaysclassroom.com/

The **Transition Region and Coronal Explorer** (TRACE) is a NASA mission to image the solar corona and transition region. TRACE Educational Resources provide the general public, specifically students and teachers, with tools to learn more about the Sun and about the TRACE program. You'll find some basic information, such as a graphical model of the Sun as well as a spectacular image gallery and set of movies.
http://vestige.lmsal.com/TRACE/

POETRY (Public Outreach, Education, Teaching and Reaching Youth) is associated with NASA's Imager for Magnetosphere-to-Auroral Global Exploration (IMAGE) satellite program. It has an extensive set of images as well as classroom activities. The project is developing classroom materials that help students understand the Earth's magnetic field, auroras, and how solar storms cause disturbances in the Earth's space environment. It's sheer poetry!
http://image.gsfc.nasa.gov/poetry/

Astronomy Café. The manager of the POETRY site, author Sten Odenwald (see book listing above) also hosts The Astronomy Café, a great web site for an introduction to astronomy, with movies, images, questions answered, astronomy articles, and lots more. The web site is also available on a CD-ROM. To grab a snack or multi-course meal—go to
http://itss.raytheon.com/cafe/

Resources (continued)

Stanford Solar Center. The Stanford Solar Center On-Line Activity Resources site is designed for the joy of solar science exploration. This site presents a collection of fun educational activities based on Solar Oscillations Investigation (SOI) and NASA's Solar and Heliospheric Observatory (SOHO) data. Students can explore the Sun's tangled magnetic field, its turbulent surface motions, the dramatic sunspot cycle, and even what happens in the solar interior where instrumental eyes cannot penetrate. The opening page includes alternating quotations about the Sun, such as: "To the best of our knowledge, our Sun is the only star proven to grow vegetables." (Philip Scherrer, 1973) For lots more, visit:
http://solar-center.stanford.edu/

The GLOBE Program. The GLOBE Program is an internet-mediated system of schools around the world dedicated to providing scientifically valid data on environmental characteristics related to weather, climate, and ecology. One of the GLOBE "Learning Investigations" is entitled *Seasons Investigation: Putting It All Together*. It is an excellent source for extensions to this GEMS unit, and for helping students come up with ideas for and methods to pursue independent investigations on their own of season-related topics. Check out:
http://www.globe.gov/

Software

Seasons Software
The Seasons software from Riverside Scientific in St. Paul, Minnesota is a powerful modeling system that allows you to change the Earth's orbit and the tilt of the Earth's axis and then predict how these changes will affect the seasons. The program is available on the CD, on a 30-day trial basis, beginning when the program is first used. We strongly encourage teachers to purchase the program as its value to this guide is significant, and it is helpful in other respects as well. The software is available in either a Mac or PC version. Students can see for themselves the effect of the tilt of the Earth's axis on seasons. The program also shows how the amount of sunlight and temperature of different places on Earth affects the seasons. Riverside has developed other excellent earth science software programs such as Winds and Clouds. Go to:
http://www.riversci.com/

Starry Night at SPACE.com
SPACE.com (http://www.space.com/) is the organization/web site which has acquired and now includes updated information on Starry Night, another excellent software program included on the CD-ROM. A *New York Times* review said, "There are few experiences as invigorating as being out in the countryside standing under a canopy of stars on a still night. Starry Night conveys that feeling better than any other desktop planetarium." For more information, updates, and free download, go to:
http://www.starrynight.com/

Literature Connections

A Circle of Seasons
by Myra Cohn Livingston
Holiday House, 1988
Although suggested for somewhat younger students, this thirteen-stanza poem following the cycle of the seasons could help encourage your students' own creative efforts.

Dear Rebecca, winter is here
by Jean Craighead George; **illustrated by Loretta Krupinski**
HarperCollinsPublishers, 1993.
A grandmother explains to her granddaughter how the arrival of winter brings changes in nature and the Earth's creatures, and how the return of spring and summer will bring more changes.

Discover the Seasons
by Diane Iverson
Dawn Publications, 1996
Poetry about the seasons with hands-on activities and recipes.

Epitaph for a Peach: Four Seasons on My Family Farm
by David Mas Masumoto
Harper, 1996
This beautifully written adult non-fiction book for more advanced readers is arranged by the seasons, as the author describes the joys, hard work, environmental and economic challenges of growing fruit in Del Rey, California.

The Four Seasons
by Antonio Vivaldi
Bullfinch Press, 1999
This book with CD includes a recording of the world-famous composition by Antonio Vivaldi. Text includes the original sonnets that inspired the music and great art to suit the seasons depicted.

Four Seasons of Corn: A Winnebago Tradition
by Sally M. Hunter
Lerner Publications, 1996
This book describes the daily life of 12-year old Russell, a middle schooler of mixed heritage experiencing the modern city of St. Paul while learning about his grandfather's Winnebago traditions, particularly the importance of corn.

A Haiku Garden: The Four Seasons in Poems and Prints
Stephen Addiss, Fumiko Yamamoto and Akira Yamamoto (editors)
Weatherhill, 1996
Season-related poetry with accompanying woodcuts. Have your students write haikus on the seasons!

The Nest: A Journal of Seasons
by Crystal Reeve
The Running Cat, 1999
This book is a photo essay of the seasons as they impact a small nest and surrounding area in Sinks Canyon State Park, Wyoming. There is space on each page for journal writing.

Nicky the Nature Detective
Ulf Svedberg, Lena Anderson (illustrator), Ingrid Selberg (translator)
Farrar Straus & Giroux, 1998
This well-known book is filled with information as, season by season, it describes changes in flora and fauna, with lots of ideas for nature activities.

The Seasons and Someone
by Virginia Kroll; illustrated by Tatsuro Kiuchi
Harcourt Brace, 1994.
A young Inuit girl in Alaska describes how the animals and her family adapt to the changing seasons.

Thirteen Moons on Turtle's Back: A Native American Year of Moons
by Joseph Bruchac, Jonathan London; illustrated by Thomas Locker.
Philomel Books/Putnam & Grosset, 1992
Stories from different Native American cultures evoke seasonal change. Among the moons are: Baby Bear Moon, Moon When Wolves Run Together, Moon of Popping Trees, and Moose-Calling Moon. The book notes that some Native American cultures, such as those in the far north and the desert, divide seasons in different ways, such as winter/summer or dry time/time of rains.

Thirteen Moons Series
by Jean Craighead George
HarperCollins, 1991/1992.
These books portray crucial episodes in the lives of animals in different seasons, organized by month. The series includes: The moon of the salamanders (1992); The moon of the chickarees (1992); The moon of the fox pups (1992); The moon of the wild pigs (1992); The moon of the mountain lions (1991); The moon of the deer 1992; The moon of the alligators (1991); The moon of the gray wolves (1991); The moon of the moles (1992); and The moon of the winter bird (1992).

To every thing there is a season: verses from Ecclesiastes
Illustrations by Leo & Diane Dillon
Blue Sky Press, 1998.
Presents the famous excerpt from Ecclesiastes and complements each verse with a different style of art from around the world.

Other Indigenous peoples have their own traditions, such as the inhabitants of the beautiful Pacific island of Pohnpei, about 2,900 miles southwest of Hawaii. An article on "The Traditional Seasons of Pohnpei" on the Astronomical Society of the Pacific web site describes the two seasons there—rahk and isol. Rakh runs from March to September, and coincides with the rainy season. It is the season of plenty, when breadfruit ripens, and five feasts during rakh honor the breadfruit. Isol runs from September to March, and is the dry season, historically a time of little food. Six feasts during isol honor different varieties of yam (there are 177 varieties on the island).

Summary Outlines

Activity 1: Name the Season

Getting Ready
Photocopy Seasons Lab Book for each student.

Introducing Seasons
1. Tell class they'll study relationships between Earth and Sun.
2. Ask, "What kinds of changes occur with the seasons?"
3. Point out categories in what they described—biological, meteorological, and sociological/cultural changes.
4. Create reference chart of seasonal changes as described in guide.
5. Tell students they'll play "Name the Season." The chart may help them.
6. Give out Seasons Lab Book. Have students write names on covers, turn to page 3, go over rules of game with them.
7. Give examples of seasonal clues, asking if students can guess.
8. Hand out blank paper. They'll have exactly five minutes. If they finish early, they can illustrate. After five minutes, have them stop.

Playing "Name the Season"
1. Tell students they'll have five minutes to read paragraphs. To get points, they write down correct season and author. Have them begin.
2. Have some or all students read paragraphs aloud before naming the season. When season is named, rest of class can check their guesses and put an "X" by each wrong guess.
3. Ask for some of students' favorite seasonal clues and add to chart.
4. Have students count number of correct guesses they made.

Activity 2: Sun-Earth Survey (Part A)

Getting Ready
1. Plug in lamp where all can gather around it. Don't need to darken room.
2. Have Earth globe handy where you will introduce the activity.

Reviewing Some Key Sun-Earth Concepts

The Earth's Shape and its Revolution Around the Sun
1. Ask: Why is the Sun important? Why did ancient peoples worship it?
2. Hold up globe. "If Earth is a ball, why does it look flat or hilly to us?"
3. Point to Australia, and ask why people there don't "fall off."
4. Turn light bulb on and room lights off. Ask how Earth moves in relation to the Sun (revolves in orbit and spins on axis). Demonstrate. Ask how long one revolution around Sun takes [one year], how long Earth takes to spin once on axis [24 hours], and how many 24 hour days in year? [365]
5. Point out model is not to scale. The Sun is much bigger and hotter than Earth, and much farther away.

Night and Day on "Mount Nose"
1. Gather students in circle around light bulb; their heads represent the Earth.
2. Ask them to imagine their nose is a mountain. A person lives on tip of "Mount Nose." Ask, "For person on Mount Nose, where in the sky is the Sun?" [high, over person's head] Ask what time of day it is [noon]
3. Continue having students turn, asking questions as in guide. At end, have students rotate through one more day.

The Sun-Earth Survey
1. Say most people understand Earth revolves around Sun once a year, and what causes day and night. Many don't understand why seasons happen.
2. Harvard graduates were asked about seasons—most had mistaken ideas. Soon your students will understand seasons better than Harvard graduates!
3. Introduce survey. Not for a grade, not a test. Later they will return to it. Have them turn in books to survey, write in ink, and be ready to explain.

Surveying Family and Friends
1. Regain attention and discuss. Urge students to share reasoning.
2. You aren't going to tell them responses that scientists would consider correct. Upcoming activities will help them figure this out for themselves!
3. They'll get two copies of survey for friends/family.
4. Pass out the surveys to be returned next session.

Part B: The Results of the Survey

Getting Ready
Plan groups of from four to six students.

Pooling the Data from Sun-Earth Surveys
1. Students take out own surveys and those completed by friends/family.
2. The goal is to come to some conclusions about what everyone surveyed thinks about seasons and the Sun-Earth connection. They'll first add up their data from the surveys in small groups with a student as recorder.
3. When everyone finishes, ask recorders for group's totals, and record. Ask volunteers to calculate grand totals and record for each question.
4. Ask students what they can conclude. Accept all responses, encouraging generalizations. "Were any results surprising to you? Why?"
5. Each student will make a graph to represent the totals for each question. Students may choose how to represent data.
6. Ask for suggestions about what information should be included on the graph, how to fit all the data onto the paper, labels needed, a title.
7. Ask students to display graphs. Did graphing help see results?
8. In next few days students will find out if the majority opinions of the class agree or disagree with responses most scientists would give.

Activity 3: Trip to the Sun

Getting Ready
1. Decide on whether you will use overhead transparencies or the CD-ROM.
2. Draw circle 28 cm in diameter by making strip as described in guide.
3. Decide if you will go outside for scale model activity at end of session.

A Trip to the Sun
1. Students will take a "trip to the Sun," starting in San Francisco at sunrise, traveling in a straight line. Ask, "Which direction is the Sun at sunrise?"
2. Students are in imaginary spaceship gradually increasing speed from hovering to hundreds of thousands kilometers per hour. Each observation point has views toward Sun and Earth, distance traveled and altitude.
3. The spaceship will not take off vertically, but horizontally, straight toward just rising Sun. Have students turn to "Trip to the Sun." Display first CD image or top half first overhead. Note view toward Sun and crescent moon.
4. Ask students to record the "Distance Traveled" and the "Altitude."
5. Start journey. For each observation point, ask: "Has the view towards the Sun changed?" "What do we see in view toward Earth?"
6. At each point, have students record "Distance Traveled," "Altitude," and (optional) "Speed." Give students a sense of altitude as described in guide.
7. At step 8, ask, "What is the diameter of Earth?"
8. Why is Moon a crescent in step 8, but nearly full in step 9? (This is a view not normally seen from Earth—it is the "far side" of the Moon.)
9. In image 9, the Moon appears to be bigger than Earth. Is it really? [No.] Why does it look bigger here? [It's closer to us.]
10. Image 10 shows sunspots; 11 shows granulation in Sun's surface; and 12 shows solar flares. The view back shows a planet Earth dot.
11. Say it's a good thing this was an imaginary trip. What would happen if we flew too close to the Sun?

Reflecting on the Trip to the Sun
1. Ask, "Did our altitude increase in first several steps? [Yes. Not much in step 2, but after that, it increased fast.]
2. Ask student to list altitudes for first six steps of journey, while you record.
3. Choose spot to represent Sun. Remind students trip didn't take off vertically. Hold globe with San Francisco facing toward Sun. Ask what time it is in San Francisco [noon]. Use ruler to show a vertical take-off.
5. Challenge class to help you use ruler and globe to show how the trip did take off. Model path as described in guide.
6. Ask, "If we were traveling in a straight line east toward the Sun, why did our altitude above the ground increase?" [Our path was a straight line, but the Earth's surface is curved—Earth is a ball. As we flew in a straight line toward the Sun, the Earth's surface curved away from us.]
7. Have students write and draw in lab books on why altitude was gained. Go around so all see ruler's farther from ground over New York than Denver.

A Sun-Earth Scale Model

1. Tell students to get a true sense of the distance from Earth to Sun they'll make a scale model.

2. If we made a scale model where 50,000 km = 1 cm, the Earth would be much smaller than the classroom globe: 0.25 cm in diameter, or about the size of a pinhead. Make a dot of about 0.25 cm on the chalkboard to represent Earth, and ask, "At this scale, how big do you think the Sun would be?" Accept some guesses, then hold up 28 cm diameter circle you cut out earlier. (Be sure students understand the Sun is a ball, like Earth.)

3. Ask "At the same scale, how far away from Earth is the Sun?"

4. Accept guesses, then say at this scale Sun is about 30 meters from Earth.

5. Explain that a meter is very roughly one "pace." Ask, "Would the scale distance to the Sun, 30 paces, fit in the classroom?" [no]

6. If feasible, invite students to go outside to pace off distance to Sun in this model. Tape paper "sun" to fence or wall. Together, walk 30 paces it. Point out that at 30 meters the paper sun looks about same size as real Sun in sky.

7. Remind students of size of Earth at this scale: about the head of a pin, with Moon a speck one quarter Earth's size, about eight meters away from Earth. Have them imagine how much bigger in scale real Sun-Earth system is.

8. Refer back to question #2 on the Sun-Earth Survey. Which drawing most accurately represents the Sun-Earth distance? [C]

9. Refer to #3 on the survey. Some people may have picked answer C but not B— but how could that be? (If some students did this, encourage them to explain reasoning.) If their response includes a reference to the Earth's tilt, ask, "Does a tilt of the Earth really make the United States closer enough in summer to make a big difference in temperature?"

Activity 4: What Shape is Earth's Orbit?

Getting Ready

1. Make the 40 cm piece of string into loop by tying the ends together so loop measures 17 cm stretched flat.

2. Make one smaller loop per student pair. Cut one 25 cm piece of string per pair. If students will tie them, you'll need to provide rulers.

3. Post piece of paper at least 14 x 14 inches. Practice drawing an ellipse before class as described in guide.

The Shape of the Earth's Orbit

1. Tell class they'll learn about the shape of the Earth's orbit around the Sun. Draw or use overhead of three orbit shapes and label as shown in guide.

2. Poll students, "Which drawing most correctly shows the shape of the Earth's orbit around the Sun: A, B, or C?"

3. Explain that an ellipse is an oval shape, a very precise and symmetrical oval. Students will draw ellipses of real orbits of Earth and Pluto. You will demonstrate how to draw an ellipse with a comet's orbit.

4. Demonstrate how to draw an ellipse as described in guide.

5. Explain that each point where push pin goes is a focus of the ellipse (plural is foci). The comet orbit is elongated, not circular. In orbits of planets (and comets or asteroids) Sun is fixed at only one of the foci of the ellipse.

6. They will draw orbits of Earth and Pluto. Show how to place open page of book on newspaper so pins won't damage desk tops.

7. Say Pluto and Earth have foci separations of 5 cm and 0.4 cm. Have students begin.

8. Have an early finisher draw Pluto and Earth orbits on transparency using two colors. In same colors, label orbits "Pluto" and "Earth."

9. When everyone is finished, collect string, newspaper, and push pins.

Dispelling a Common Misconception About Earth's Orbit

1. Project overhead of Earth's and Pluto's orbits. Ask, "Is Earth's orbit really larger than Pluto's?" [No, it's actually much smaller.] Remind them that we are concentrating here only on the *shapes* of the orbits.

2. Ask, "Which orbit is more circular, Pluto's or Earth's?" [Earth's] Explain that while Earth's orbit is slightly elliptical, it is very nearly circular. Pluto has the least circular orbit of all the planets, and it still looks pretty circular. Comet orbits are more elongated.

3. Have class look back at the results and graphs from question #1 on the survey: "Which of the four drawings do you think best shows the shape of Earth's orbit around the Sun?

4. Ask, "Did many people choose answer C or D?" "What is wrong with those answers?"

5. Ask students where Sun should be in drawings of Earth's and Pluto's orbits. [the center] Reveal that, not only is Earth's orbit almost circular, the Sun is in the center of the orbit. So, of question #1's answers, A and B, which is correct? [A] Distance from Earth to the Sun does not change much relative to the entire distance. Earth is actually closest to the Sun on January 4!

6. Ask students why they think many people pick C or D. [Drawings in books often make orbits look like skinny ellipses and are often drawn from the side] Use a hula hoop or large embroidery hoop to demonstrate,

7. Tell students that if you ask people, "What causes seasons?" most of them say, "The Earth is closer to the Sun in summer, farther from the Sun in winter." Many people thus choose answers B, C, or D.

8. Remind students of Question 3—Why is it hotter in New York in June than December?" Ask how many people the class surveyed picked answer B. Emphasize that being closer to the Sun is **not** why we have summer.

Activity 5: Temperatures Around the World

Getting Ready

1. Make overhead of "Temperatures Around the World" graphing sheet and Temperature Graph. Color code temperature lines. Make overhead of Temperature Sample Data.

2. Check if students know how to find locations by latitude and longitude.

Temperatures Around the World

1. Ask students to think back to "Name the Season" game. One thing they mentioned often was temperature.

2. Project Globe measures temperatures around world. Students will consider how temperatures change in different seasons and parts of world.

3. Project overhead about El Salvador. They'll get data from nine places. Show how it is arranged. Emphasize these are *monthly* average temperatures.

Longitude and Latitude

1. Hold up globe, and point out the longitude lines that run vertically.
2. Ask volunteer to trace equator. Set of lines that goes around globe horizontally are latitude lines.
3. On maps and globes, lines of latitude and longitude are in degrees.
4. Project world map; again point out longitude and latitude.
5. On map, show that equator is 0° latitude; each line to north adds five degrees until North Pole (90° north latitude). Going south from equator, each latitude increases by 5 degrees, and South Pole is 90° south. Emphasize importance of saying north or south along with degrees of latitude.
6. Say longitude lines go from 0° to 180° and increase 5° to east and west.
7. Demonstrate how to find Chalatenango, El Salvador on world map using its latitude (14° north) and longitude (89° west).
8. Have students locate, mark, label the nine cities on their world maps.

Graphing Temperatures Around the World

1. Tell class that they will look at the temperature in nine places on Earth they've just located. Data is in lab books.
2. Scientists all over world use Celsius temperature scale. There is a conversion table in lab books. Have students use the table to find freezing point of water and normal human temperature in both C and F scales.
3. Project blank Temperature Graph. Demonstrate how to plot temperature average of 12°C in January. Lines on graph are two degrees apart. Students need to know negative numbers, and how to plot temperatures below zero.
4. Ask, "What do you think the graph would look like in our area over the time period from January to June?" (Average temperature will rise.) "What would happen after that?" (Average temperature will fall.)
5. Ask, "Does temperature have the same pattern as ours all over the world?" By graphing temperatures, they can find out if seasons differ.
6. If your students need practice, plot average temperatures for Chalatenango together. Then assign students to plot average temperatures for as many cities as they can, connecting the data points with a smooth line.

Analyzing the Temperature Graphs

1. After all students have plotted at least three cities, ask, "What have we found out? " "What patterns do you see?"
2. Make sure they notice that pattern is reversed between North and South. In North, hottest months are June–August; in South, hottest months are December–February. Ask, "What season is it where we live in July?" (Summer) "What season is it in Antarctica in July?" (Winter)
3. Ask, "What is the pattern of temperature change for locations near the equator?" [Not much variation in temperature through all seasons.]
4. Remind students of question #3 in Sun-Earth Survey. What do they think of answer B given what they observed on graphs?

Activity 6: Days and Nights Around the World

Getting Ready
1. Make overhead of Day Length Graph.
2. Make overhead of completed Day Length Graph and color code.
3. Make overhead of sample "Day Length" data in guide.

Hours of Daylight
1. Have the students think back to Activity 1. How many wrote about changes in "length of day?"
2. Ask questions to review changes in the number of daylight hours, such as: Does the Sun always set at the same time each day? [No]. At what times of year does the Sun stay up latest (and rise the earliest)? [Summer. Don't reveal the answer if no one knows.] Is the number of hours of daylight the same each day?" [No] When are the "shortest days?" [Winter]
3. Ask, "Is the number of hours of daylight on a certain day the same all over the world?" Students will look at data from around the world.
4. Display and explain sample "Day Length" data for Latitude 38 degrees north on the overhead. This data is in lab book, plus data for more locations. Model how to graph day length for one of the latitudes.
6. Have students graph as many of the "Day Length" values from the eight latitudes as they can, color coding plot lines for each latitude.
7. The first two latitudes they plot should be in opposite hemispheres.
8. Have students proceed; save at least ten minutes for discussion.

Discussing the "Day Length" Graphs
1. Regain the attention of the class.
2. Put the "Day Length" graph transparency on the overhead. Ask, "What patterns do you see?"
3. Point to the Ecuador data. Ask, "If the data makes a straight horizontal line across the graph, what does that say about how the length of day changes at that latitude?" [Day length stays same all year.] Ask, "What do the lines that go up and down steeply tell you?" [At that latitude, day length changes greatly with the seasons.]
4. Be sure students notice that locations at opposite latitudes in northern and southern hemispheres have day lengths which are mirror images of each other. Ask, "What season is it in Scotland in July?" [summer] "What season is it in New Zealand in July?" [winter] Students should be able to perceive a high degree of symmetry and that each plot line is highly symmetrical on either side of the month of June.
5. Ask, "Are there any places where the Sun never comes up certain parts of the year?" [Yes. Antarctica, Alaska, Norway, Canada] At what times of year does that happen? [At opposite times in far north and far south.)
6. "Where and when does Sun stay up for 24 hours?" [Sun never sets from May through July above 70°N latitude (Alaska); also November through January at latitudes south of 70° S.(Antarctica) This is sometimes called the "midnight Sun."]
7. If no one points out that all the lines converge at two points, ask, "Are there any places where all the lines come together?" [Yes, in March and September] "What seasons are these?" [spring and fall]

8. Say there is a special name for exact date where all lines come together, when number of daylight hours equals number of night hours. Ask if anyone know term for those special days[Equinoxes—Spring equinox and fall or autumnal equinox] They occur near March 21 and September 21 each year.

9. Remind students of question #3 in survey. Ask, "Do your observations about the number of daylight hours help you rule out any of the answers?"

10. Tell the class the next activity will make clear for them why the day length changes with the seasons the way it does.

Activity 7: Tilted Earth

Getting Ready
1. The room needs to be darkened.
2. Set up the light bulb above eye level near center of room.
3. Mark polystyrene balls with different colors as detailed in guide.

Introducing the Model
1. Ask students to remember the shape of Earth's orbit they drew. Does Earth's distance from Sun change much during the year? [no]

2. If Earth did move closer or farther from the Sun, it would be colder or hotter everywhere on Earth at the same time. Ask, "Is it summer at the same time everywhere on Earth? [no—in last two activities, summer and winter happen at same time in different parts of world.]

3. Ask, "If it's not the distance to the Sun that causes seasons, what are some other possible causes?" If students don't refer to Earth's tilt, mention it.

4. Tell class they'll make a Sun-Earth model. Sun will be a light bulb; sphere the Earth. Show how to put sphere on pencil to spin it. This represents Earth rotating on "spin axis" from North to South Pole.

A Model with No Tilt
1. Hand out model Earths. Have each student put pencil into sphere. Gather everyone around light bulb, turn off room lights.

2. Ask students to find on spheres the Equator and North Pole, and Northern and Southern Hemispheres. Identify other marks—green dot: mid-latitude in Northern Hemisphere. Blue dot: high-latitude in Northern Hemisphere. Black dot: mid-latitude in Southern Hemisphere.

3. Have students hold Earth models with the spin axis vertical, slowly spin them, and watch dot cities move from daylight into night and back again. Ask, "With your pencil (spin axis) vertical, do the blue, green, and black dots stay in the light the same amount of time (daytime)?" [Yes, roughly]

4. Ask, "Is this really how the Sun-Earth system works?" [No. The spin axis should be tilted.] Have students tilt Earth toward Sun—at about 45° angle. (Real angle is 23.5°, but OK to exaggerate for now.)

5. Have students spin Earth again and watch dots. Ask them to compare the green dot and black dot cities. Do they both get day and night? [yes, but the city in the Northern Hemisphere has long days and short nights, while in the Southern Hemisphere, there are long nights and short days.]

6. Ask, "How about the blue dot—does it have day and night?" [No. It receives light the whole 24 hours; it has midnight Sun.] What is happening near the South Pole? [24 hours of darkness]

7. Have students compare what is happening in the two Northern Hemisphere cities. What season is it in the green dot city? The blue dot? [both have summer] How are they different? [Day length longer in blue dot city.]
8. All their Northern Hemispheres are tilted toward Sun, and have summer. Is this how it always is? How does the season change from summer to fall, winter, and spring during the year? Does the Earth rock back and forth? [no]

Tilting the Earth Toward the North Star
1. Tell students that, as the Earth moves around the Sun, the North Pole always points at North Star.
2. Pick a spot as North Star. Have students tilt North Pole of spheres toward it, and spin spheres with North Pole pointed at North Star.
3. Check that students between Sun and North Star are keeping North Poles tilted away from Sun, toward North Star. Students on opposite side of "orbit" should have North Poles tilted toward Sun (and North Star). Students midway between have North Pole pointing "sideways" to Sun.
4. Stand near students whose North Poles are tilted toward Sun. Ask, "When the Earth is in this part of its orbit, which Hemisphere is tilted more toward the Sun?" [Northern.] "Is it the same season in Northern and Southern Hemispheres?" [No. In northern it's summer, in southern it's winter.]
5. Move counterclockwise around circle of students stopping at 1/4 of the way around, halfway around, and 3/4 of the way around. At each stop, ask, "For the model Earths in this part of the orbit, is the North Pole pointing toward or away from Sun?" [At 1/4 and 3/4 stops answer is neither—it's pointing "sideways" to the Sun.] "What season is this?" [1st stop it's fall in Northern Hemisphere; spring in Southern Hemisphere; 2nd stop it's winter in Northern Hemisphere and summer in Southern Hemisphere; 3rd stop it's spring in Northern Hemisphere and fall in Southern Hemisphere.]
6. Point to students with North Poles tilted toward Sun—the Northern Hemisphere's summer position. Ask, "If Norway and Alaska are watching the Midnight Sun, what do people see in Antarctica?" (Stars, 24-hour nights.)
7. Review by asking students to raise hands if their Earth position has: longer days at South Pole; longer days at North Pole; day length about the same in both hemispheres.

A Rotating Tilted Earth
Ask students to rotate model Earths until "hometown" (red dot) is at noontime. In which season is the Sun highest in the sky at noon?" [summer]

A Revolving Earth
1. Define hand symbols for four seasons as described in guide.
2. Add revolution of Earth around Sun. Have students walk around (orbit) the Sun, making sure their Earth axes ALWAYS point to the North Star.
3. Have students stop 1/4 way around circle. Check that axes are still pointing to North Star. Have students hold up hand symbol.
4. Repeat step 3 two more times so students have opportunity to give the hand symbol for each season, for a complete annual cycle.
5. Collect spheres, turn on the room lights, have students return to seats.

Discussing the Model and What Causes Seasons

1. Ask students to write down what they learned about the causes of seasons. Ask a few students to explain what they learned from the model.
2. Ask, "Do you think a planet whose axis was not tilted at all would have seasons?"
3. Say many people think tilt of Earth causes seasons because it makes one part of Earth closer to the Sun. Ask, "When North Pole is tilted toward the Sun, is Northern Hemisphere much closer to the Sun than the Southern Hemisphere?" [No—a few thousand kilometers is not significant compared with the nearly 15 million kilometers distance from Earth to Sun.]
4. Remind them of scale model in Activity 3—if Earth were the size of a pinhead, the Sun would be a 28 cm beach ball thirty meters away. Ask, "Does it make much difference in the 30 meter distance to the Sun if the pinhead is tilted?" [no] Emphasize distance from Earth to Sun is enormous.
5. If tilt doesn't make difference in distance from Sun, why hotter in summer? [More daylight hours. Angle makes light more concentrated, but don't reveal unless student mentions.] They'll explore more next session.
6. Refer to #3 on survey. Which answers supported by model they made?

Activity 8: The Angle of Sunlight/Seasons Unraveled

Getting Ready
1. Set up the 100 watt light as in the previous activity.
2. Photocopy Light Angle Analyzers onto heavy cardstock.
3. Familiarize yourself with how to use the Light Angle Analyzer.

The Angle of Sunlight
1. Tell class they now understand more about seasons than many college graduates, but there is one more issue before they're experts. They will consider how high the Sun gets in the sky during different seasons.
2. Turn on light bulb-model Sun or use point on wall as Sun. Hold up globe, and point out your location in Northern Hemisphere. Tilt Northern Hemisphere toward Sun. Ask, "What season is it where we live?" [summer] Spin globe so location is facing Sun. "What time is it?" [noon]
3. Keep Earth in summer noon position. Hold up ruler as ray of sunlight from Sun to Earth in summer. Say light travels in a straight line. Place one end of ruler on location, and other end toward Sun. Ask, "To someone at this point on Earth, would the Sun appear high or low in the sky?"
4. Ask how Earth is tilted in winter. Walk to other side of Sun and tilt Northern Hemisphere away from Sun, but spin it so your location faces Sun. Point out that where ruler "sunlight ray" strikes is now a very shallow angle.
5. Help students see that Sun seems to be overhead in summer, but lower in sky in winter. For each position, ask, "Where in the sky does the Sun seem to be?" [high overhead at noon in summer, lower in sky at noon in winter]

Introducing the Sun Angle Analyzer

1. Tell the students that they get to use a "Sun Angle Analyzer" to see what happens when light hits the ground at different angles.
2. Demonstrate how to stick a paper fastener (brad) through the x-mark just above the "window" hole as described in guide.
3. Explain that they'll use the analyzer with a partner. Hand out a Sun Angle Analyzer and fastener to each pair. Once fasteners in place, gather around light bulb. Turn off the room lights and close blinds.
4. Ignoring the protractor part for now, practice using the analyzers together. Call their attention to the instructions written on the Light Angle Analyzers.
5. Regain attention of group, and ask what they have noticed. [As ground moves up closer to window, fewer grid squares are covered by light. Light seems brighter when fewer squares are covered.]
6. If students won't make angle measurements, skip this step and next. If they are, show use of protractor for measuring angle of light hitting ground.
7. Tell them to find angle of light when spread over 4, 6, and all grid squares.
8. When students finish, collect analyzers and students return to seats.

Discussing the Light Analyzer Results

1. Ask for angle of light when only four squares were filled with light. [90°]
2. Ask for the light angle when six grid squares were filled with light. [answers may vary] What about when all grid squares were filled? [small angle] A knowledge that variation in answers may be due to imprecision of the instrument and inaccuracies in measurement.
3. Ask if students noticed any changes in how bright the light looked.
4. Tell students when light is more concentrated, ground gets hotter. Help them relate their discoveries with light analyzers to Earth's seasons.

Seasons Unraveled

1. Have students take the Seasons Survey again, or go over it together now.
2. Ask what they now think about question #3. Discuss, referring back to the unit's activities. If they pick C, remind them the United States *is* tilted toward Sun in June, so is a bit closer, but that doesn't change the distance from Sun enough to make it hotter due to the change in distance.
3. Explain that Earth's axis is tilted by about 23° with respect to its orbit around the Sun. The spin axes of other planets have different tilt angles. Uranus' is nearly 90°! Ask students what seasons might be like on Uranus.
4. Discuss ways increased heat and more daylight hours (or vice versa) lead to greater or less plant growth, fit in with organism life cycles, affect the weather, etc. to influence all the phenomena we call "the seasons."
5. Ask students if they have additional questions or issues to raise.
6. Summarize by saying that the main causes of the seasonal changes on Earth derive from what astronomers call a Sun-Earth connection.
7. Praise students for their scientific work! Suggest that students explain the correct survey responses and real reasons for seasons to their families and friends.

Some Rhymes for All Seasons (by L.B.)

*If you do share any or all of these seasons rhymes with your class, do so **only** after they have completed all the activities in the guide!*

The seasons come and then they go
Do you know what makes it so?
Can you explain the reasons why
The seasons come and then pass by?

Many people think they know
The reason seasons come and go
Think distance 'twixt the Sun and Earth
Is what gives rise to seasons' birth.

But we have learned real reasons why
The Sun seems higher in the sky
Our thoughts now tend in right direction
Far past most common misconception

For though Earth's orbit is elliptical
Its eccentricity's not critical
Small shift in distance can't account
For temperature's decline and mount!

Seasons in North Hemisphere
Stand distance thesis on its ear—
When Sun's most close there's wintry clime
But South Pole's having summertime!

The seasons come and then they wilt
It has to do with the Earth's tilt
The angle of the Sun's bright light
The Sun and Earth's connected flight!

And something else of major note
Be we in swimsuit or warm coat—
Without the seasons as they are
We'd not be living with this star!

Name: _____

The Real Reasons for Seasons:
Sun-Earth Connections

Great Explorations
in Math and Science (GEMS)

Seasons
Lab
Book

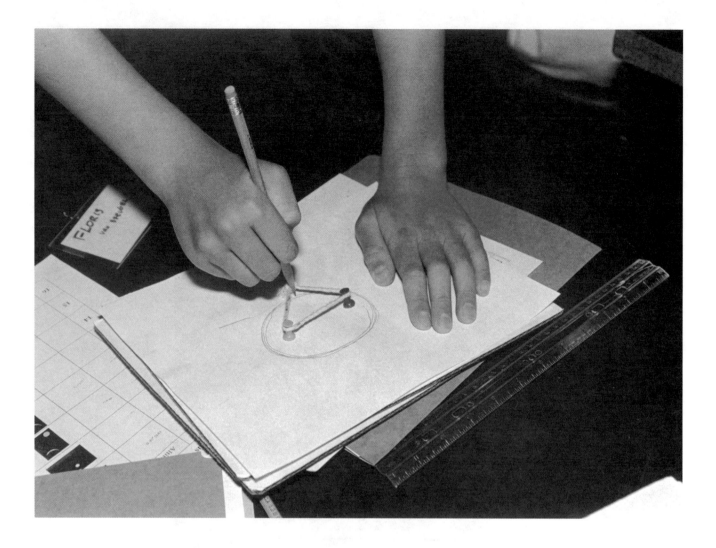

The seasons come
And then they go
Do you know
What makes it so?

1. "Name the Season" Game

Rules:

a. Pick one season to write about. On a piece of paper, write your name, but *not* the name of the season.

b. Write a paragraph describing some events, and include clues about what season it is. Without actually naming the season, make it possible for the reader to figure out what season it is.

c. At a "Ready-Set-Go" signal, leave your paragraph on your desk, and pick up a pencil and your Seasons Lab Book. Walk around and read as many of the paragraphs as possible, guessing what season each refers to.

d. For each paragraph, write below the name of the person who wrote it and which season you think is being described.

e. The person with the most correct guesses wins the game.

Student Name	Season	Student Name	Season

Sun-Earth Survey

1. **Which of the four drawings do you think best shows the shape of Earth's orbit around the Sun? (The view is top down.) Circle the correct letter.**

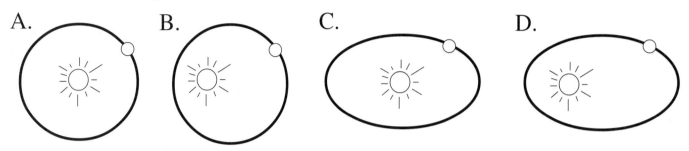

A. B. C. D.

2. **Which is the best drawing to show the sizes and distances between the Earth and the Sun? Circle the letter of the best drawing.**

A. O Earth   o Moon   (Sun)
_____

B. o Earth   o Moon   (Sun)
_____

C. ∘ Earth   · Moon   Sun is about 11 page-widths away ⟶
_____

3. **Why do you think it is hotter in the United States in June than in December? Circle all that are correct.**

A. Because the Sun itself gives off more heat and light energy in June and less in December.

B. Because the Earth is closer to the Sun in June, and farther away from the Sun in December.

C. Because the United States is closer to the Sun in June and farther from the Sun in December.

D. Because the United States is facing more toward the Sun in June and away from the Sun in December.

E. Because the Sun gets higher in the sky in June, so its rays are more concentrated on the ground.

F. Because the Moon blocks out the Sun more in December.

G. Because in the United States, there are more hours of daylight in June than in December.

3. A Trip to the Sun

Step 1

View towards Sun:

Distance _____

Altitude _____

View toward Earth:

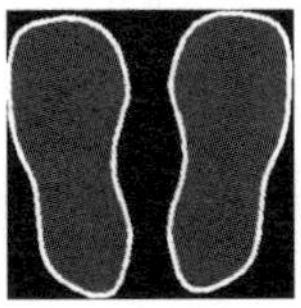

San Francisco, California

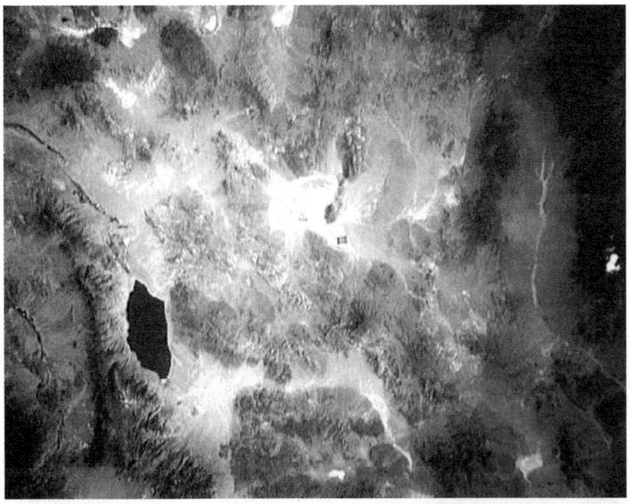

Step 2

View towards Sun:

Distance _____

Altitude _____

View toward Earth:

Sacramento, California

Step 3

View towards Sun:

Distance _____

Altitude _____

View toward Earth:

Walker Lake, Nevada

Step 4

View towards Sun:

Distance _____

Altitude _____

View toward Earth:

Denver, Colorado

A Trip to the Sun (page 2)

Step 5

View towards Sun:

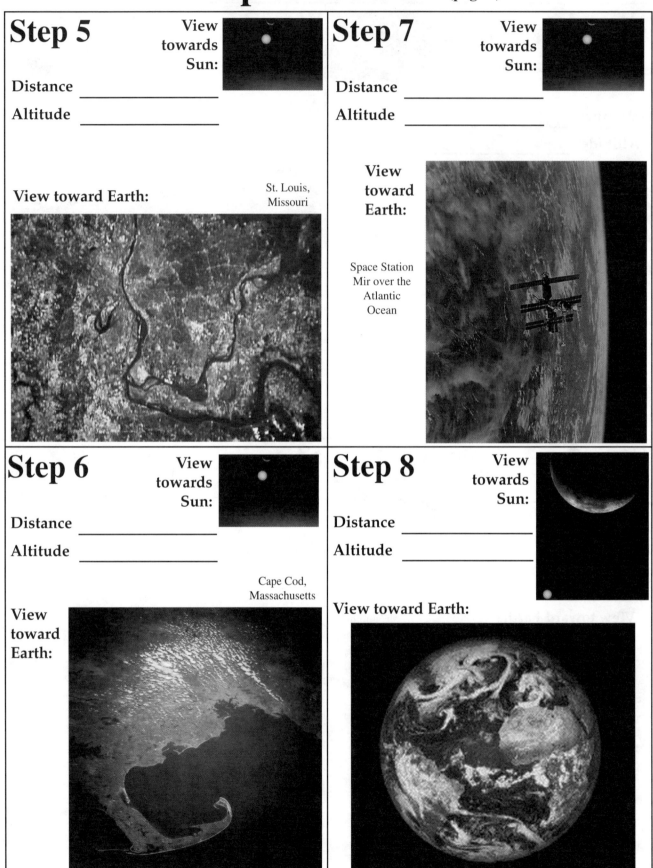

Distance _____

Altitude _____

View toward Earth:

St. Louis, Missouri

Step 6

View towards Sun:

Distance _____

Altitude _____

Cape Cod, Massachusetts

View toward Earth:

Step 7

View towards Sun:

Distance _____

Altitude _____

View toward Earth:

Space Station Mir over the Atlantic Ocean

Step 8

View towards Sun:

Distance _____

Altitude _____

View toward Earth:

A Trip to the Sun (page 3)

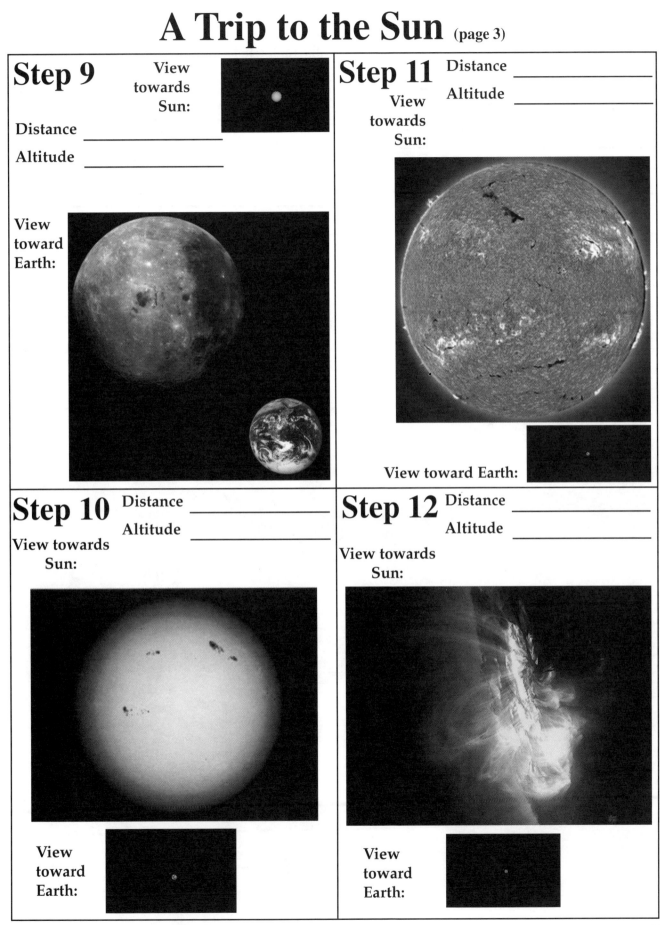

Step 9

View towards Sun:

Distance _____

Altitude _____

View toward Earth:

Step 11

Distance _____

Altitude _____

View towards Sun:

View toward Earth:

Step 10

Distance _____

Altitude _____

View towards Sun:

View toward Earth:

Step 12

Distance _____

Altitude _____

View towards Sun:

View toward Earth:

3. Trip to the Sun

Explain on this page why, even though we traveled in a straight line east toward the Sun, our altitude was increasing in the first several steps. Draw a diagram to help show your reasoning.

_____

_____

_____

_____

_____

_____

_____

_____

_____

_____

4. What Shape Is Earth's Orbit?

Draw the *shape* of...   Earth's orbit: Separation of foci = 0.4 cm

Pluto's orbit: Separation of foci = 5 cm

Which orbit seems most circular?

[Note: the *size* of these orbits would be much different in a proper scale drawing, but the *shape* of orbit is all we are looking at here.]

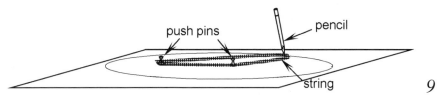

5. Temperatures Around the World Latitude and Longitude Data

Latitudes, Longitudes, and Elevations

Guangzhou, China Guangdong Guangya MS Latitude: 23°N Longitude: 113°E Elevation: 20 m	Kyoto, Japan Koryu JrHS Latitude: 36°N Longitude: 135° E Elevation: 8 m	Minnesota USA Detroit Lakes Mid Sch Lat:47°N Long:96°W Elevation: 1431 m	Kodiak, Alaska, USA Kodiak HS Latitude: 58°N Longitude: 152°W Elevation : 35 m	
Escuela Antarctica, Esperanza; Provincial #38 Julio Argentina Roca Latitude: 63°S Longitude: 57°W Elevation: 10 m	Sandy Bay,Australia Fahan School Latitude: 43°S Longitude: 147°E Elevation: 20 m	Carltonville, S Africa; Tsitsiboga Primary School Lat:26°S Long:27°E Elevation : 1524 m	Quito, Ecuador; Colegio Albert Einstein Lat:0°N Long:78°W Elevation: 2890 m	Chalatenango, El Salvador; Escuela Rural Mixta Latitude: 14°N Longitude: 89°W Elevation: 1700 m

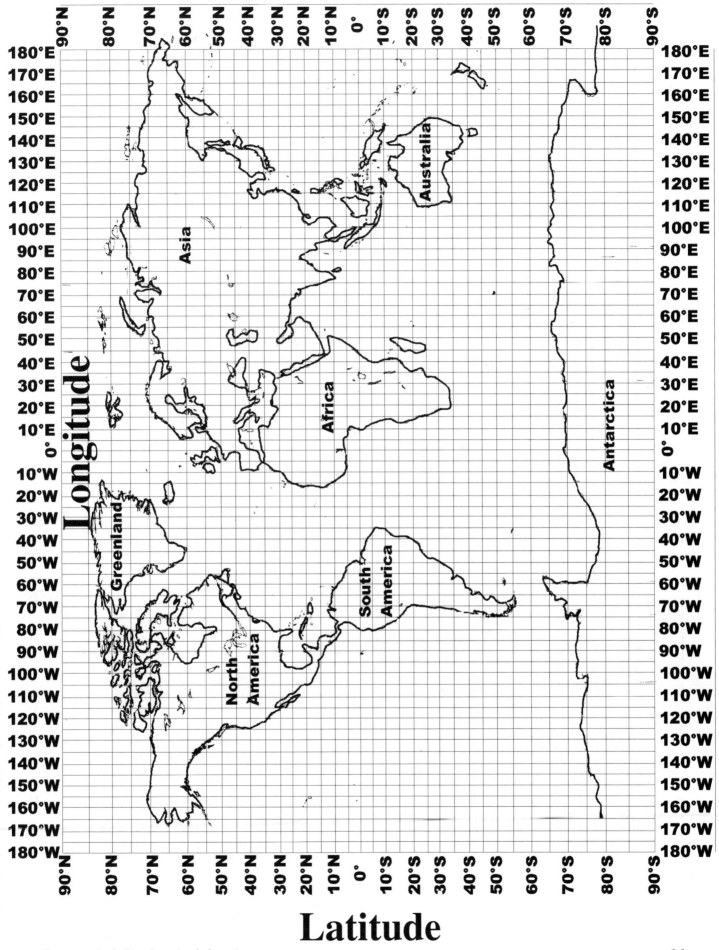

Longitude

Latitude

5. Temperatures Around the World
Average Temperatures: 1996-1998 Data from GLOBE Schools Around the World

Data is in Degrees Celsius (°C)

Below are Celsius to Fahrenheit Temperature Conversions

$$°F = (°C \times 9/5) + 32$$

°C	°F
-40	-40.0
-18	-0.4
-16	3.2
-14	6.8
-12	10.4
-10	14.0
-8	17.6
-6	21.2
-4	24.8
-2	28.4
0	32.0
2	35.6
4	39.2
6	42.8
8	46.4
10	50.0
12	53.6
14	57.2
16	60.8
18	64.4
20	68.0
22	71.6
24	75.2
26	78.8
28	82.4
30	86.0
32	89.6
34	93.2
36	96.8
38	100.4
40	104.0
100	212.0

Escuela Antarctica, Esperanza;
Provincial #38 Julio Argentina Roca
Latitude: 63° S
Longitude: 57° W
Elevation: 10 m

Month	Year	Avg Temp
May	1998	-3.9
Jun	1998	-4.2
Jul	1998	-12.5
Aug	1998	-11.5
Apr	1998	3.8
Sep	1998	-9.7
Oct	1998	-6.3
Nov	1998	0.6
Dec	1998	1.2

Quito, Ecuador;
Colegio Albert Einstein
Lat:0° N   Long:78° W
Elevation: 2890 m

Month	Year	Avg Temp
Jan	1998	18.8
Feb	1998	18.4
Mar	1998	17.6
Apr	1998	16.0
May	1998	19.7
Jun	1998	17.1
{ Aug	1997	17.6}
{ Sep	1997	18.4}
{ Oct	1997	18.0}
Nov	1997	18.3
Dec	1997	16.7

Kyoto, Japan
Koryu JrHS
Latitude: 36° N
Longitude: 135° E
Elevation: 8 m

Month	Year	Avg Temp
Jan	1996	4.4
Feb	1996	2.9
Mar	1996	6.9
Apr	1996	9.5
May	1996	16.4
Jun	1996	21.2
Jul	1996	24.3
Aug	1996	25.5
Sep	1996	20.2
Oct	1996	15.7
Nov	1995	10.3
Dec	1995	5.8

Sandy Bay, Australia
Fahan School
Latitude: 43° S
Longitude: 147° E
Elevation: 20 m

Month	Year	Avg Temp
{ Jan	1998	18.0}
Feb	1998	17.5
Mar	1998	17.9
Apr	1998	14.7
May	1998	12.8
Jun	1998	10.1
Jul	1998	11.0
Aug	1998	10.6
Sep	1998	15.2
Oct	1998	13.7
Nov	1998	14.6

Chalatenango, El Salvador;
Escuela Rural Mixta
Latitude: 14° N
Longitude: 89° W
Elevation: 1700 m

Month	Year	Avg Temp
Feb	1997	15.4
Mar	1997	15.5
Apr	1997	15.3
May	1997	16.0
Jun	1997	15.7
Jul	1997	15.7
Aug	1997	16.3
Sep	1997	16.5
Oct	1997	16.9
Dec	1996	15.1

Minnesota USA
Detroit Lakes Middle School
Lat:47° N   Long:96° W
Elevation: 1431 m

Month	Year	Avg Temp
Jan	1997	-14.1
Feb	1997	-9.2
Mar	1997	-2.1
Apr	1997	2.8
May	1997	10.6
Jun	1997	20.3
Jul	1997	19.3
Aug	1997	18.9
Sep	1997	17.3
Oct	1997	3.8
Nov	1997	-5.5
Dec	1997	-4.5

Carltonville, S Africa;
Tsitsiboga Primary School
Lat:26° S Long:27° E
Elevation : 1524 m

Month	Year	Avg Temp
Feb	1998	20.8
Mar	1998	25.2
Apr	1998	23.5
May	1998	18.9
Jun	1998	11.8
Jul	1998	13.9
Sep	1998	14.8
Oct	1998	18.8
Nov	1998	19.1

Guangzhou, China
Guangdong Guangya MS
Latitude: 23° N
Longitude: 113° E
Elevation: 20 m

Month	Year	Avg Temp
Jan	1999	13.7
Feb	1998	18.4
Mar	1998	18.5
Apr	1998	23.6
May	1998	24.8
Jun	1998	27.2
Jul-Aug	{ no data}	
Sep	1998	27.2
Oct	1998	23.1
Nov	1998	22.2
Dec	1998	18.0

Kodiak, Alaska, USA
Kodiak High School
Latitude: 58° N
Longitude: 152° W
Elevation : 35 m

Month	Year	Avg Temp
Jan	1999	-0.9
May	1998	6.4
Jun	1998	10.8
Jul	1998	12.8
Aug	1998	12.9
Sep	1998	9.9
Oct	1998	5.3
Nov	1998	2.7
Dec	1998	-1.5

5. Temperatures Around the World

Label each plot line:
a. latitude and
b. state/country

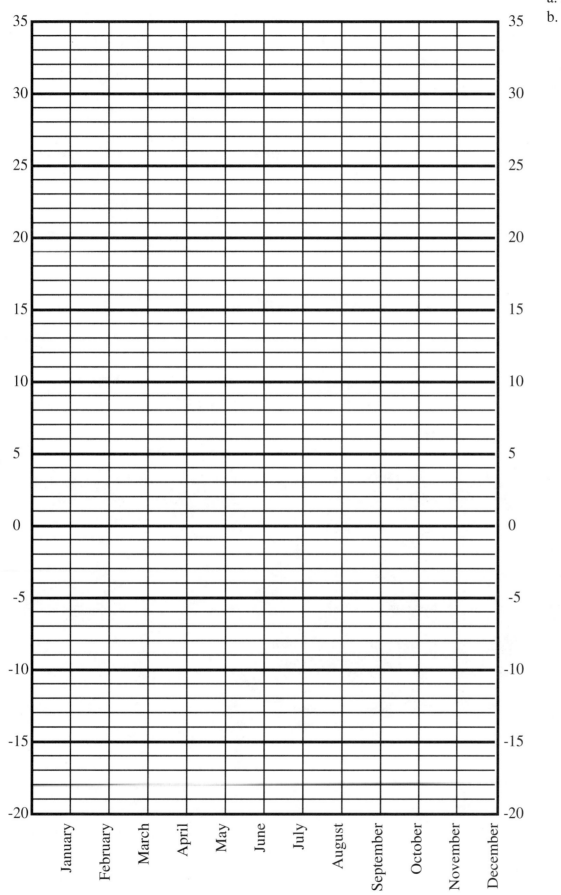

Latitude: 70° North

Date	Sunrise (AM)	Sunset (PM)	Day Length
Jan	NONE	NONE	0
Feb	8:14	4:34	8:20
Mar	6:04	6:32	12:28
Apr	3:35	8:46	17:11
May	NONE	NONE	24:00
Jun	NONE	NONE	24:00
Jul	NONE	NONE	24:00
Aug	3:36	8:46	17:10
Sep	5:46	6:17	12:31
Oct	7:49	3:58	8:09
Nov	NONE	NONE	0
Dec	NONE	NONE	0

Tromsö, NORWAY
Prudhoe Bay, ALASKA, USA
Clyde, Baffin Island, CANADA

Latitude: 57° North

Date	Sunrise (AM)	Sunset (PM)	Day Length
Jan	8:28	4:15	7:47
Feb	7:23	5:25	10:02
Mar	6:09	6:26	12:17
Apr	4:50	7:25	14:35
May	3:41	8:24	16:43
Jun	3:15	9:08	17:53
Jul	3:48	8:43	16:55
Aug	4:49	7:35	14:46
Sep	5:53	6:12	12:19
Oct	6:56	4:52	9:56
Nov	8:04	3:47	7:43
Dec	8:47	3:29	6:42

Kodiak, ALASKA, USA
Glasgow, SCOTLAND
Copenhagen, DENMARK
Moscow, RUSSIA

Latitude: 38° North

Date	Sunrise (AM)	Sunset (PM)	Day Length
Jan	7:22	5:21	9:59
Feb	6:52	5:55	11:03
Mar	6:12	6:23	12:11
Apr	5:26	6:51	13:25
May	4:55	7:18	14:23
Jun	4:47	7:36	14:49
Jul	5:04	7:28	14:24
Aug	5:30	6:55	13:25
Sep	5:57	6:08	12:11
Oct	6:24	5:24	11:00
Nov	6:57	4:54	9:57
Dec	7:22	4:54	9:32

USA: San Franci sco, CALIFORNIA
    Charleston, W. VIRGINIA
    Wichita, KANSAS   Louisville, KENTUCKY
    St. Louis, MISSOURI   Pueblo, COLORADO
                             Richmond, VIRGINIA
        Sendai, JAPAN   Seoul, S. KOREA
        Tientsin, CHINA   Izmir, TURKEY
        Athens, GREECE   Palermo, SICILY
14   Cordoba, SPAIN   Lisbon, PORTUGAL

6. Days and Nights Around the World:
Seasonal Changes in Number of Hours of Daylight
All dates are the 21th day of the month

Latitude: 26° North

Date	Sunrise (AM)	Sunset (PM)	Day Length
Jan	6:58	5:44	10:46
Feb	6:41	6:06	11:25
Mar	6:12	6:22	12:10
Apr	5:41	6:36	12:55
May	5:21	6:52	13:31
Jun	5:19	7:05	13:46
Jul	5:30	7:02	13:32
Aug	5:45	6:40	12:55
Sep	5:58	6:07	12:09
Oct	6:12	5:37	11:25
Nov	6:32	5:19	10:47
Dec	6:53	5:23	10:30

Monterey, MEXICO   Taipei, TAIWAN
Kunming CHINA   Patna, INDIA
Karachi, PAKISTAN Riyadh, SAUDI ARABIA
Luxor, EGYPT   Wau El Kebir, LIBYA

Latitude: 0°

Date	Sunrise (AM)	Sunset (PM)	Day Length
Jan	6:18	6:25	12:07
Feb	6:20	6:27	12:07
Mar	6:14	6:20	12:06
Apr	6:05	6:12	12:07
May	6:03	6:10	12:07
Jun	6:08	6:15	12:07
Jul	6:13	6:20	12:07
Aug	6:09	6:16	12:07
Sep	6:00	6:06	12:06
Oct	5:51	5:58	12:07
Nov	5:52	5:59	12:07
Dec	6:04	6:12	12:08

Quito, ECUADOR; Nairobi, KENYA;
Singapore, MALAYA

Latitude: 26° South

Date	Sunrise (AM)	Sunset (PM)	Day Length
Jan	5:36	7:06	13:30
Feb	5:59	6:48	12:49
Mar	6:14	6:20	12:06
Apr	6:28	5:48	11:20
May	6:44	5:29	10:45
Jun	6:56	5:27	10:31
Jul	6:54	5:38	10:44
Aug	6:33	5:53	11:20
Sep	6:00	6:05	12:05
Oct	5:29	6:20	12:51
Nov	5:11	6:41	13:30
Dec	5:15	7:01	13:46

Pretoria, SOUTH AFRICA
Curitiba, BRAZIL
Brisbane, AUSTRALIA
Asuncion, PARAGUAY

Latitude: 38° South

Date	Sunrise (AM)	Sunset (PM)	Day Length
Jan	5:11	7:31	14:20
Feb	5:46	7:00	13:14
Mar	6:14	6:20	12:06
Apr	6:42	5:34	10:52
May	7:09	5:04	9:55
Jun	7:26	4:47	9:21
Jul	7:19	5:13	9:54
Aug	6:47	5:39	10:52
Sep	6:01	6:05	12:04
Oct	5:16	6:33	13:17
Nov	4:45	7:07	14:22
Dec	4:44	7:32	14:48

Melbourne, AUSTRALIA
Auckland, NEW ZEALAND
Bahia Blanca, ARGENTINA
Curacautin, CHILE

Latitude: 70° South

Date	Sunrise (AM)	Sunset (PM)	Day Length
Jan	NONE	NONE	24:00
Feb	4:09	8:35	16:26
Mar	6:10	6:21	12:11
Apr	8:19	3:57	7:38
May	NONE	NONE	0
Jun	NONE	NONE	0
Jul	NONE	NONE	0
Aug	8:24	4:03	7:39
Sep	6:00	6:07	12:07
Oct	3:37	8:15	16:38
Nov	NONE	NONE	24:00
Dec	NONE	NONE	24:00

ANTARCTICA

> Data generated with Voyager
> by Carina software,
> Hayward, California

6. Days and Nights Around the World: Seasonal Changes in Number of Hours of Daylight

Label each plot line:
a. latitude and
b. state/country

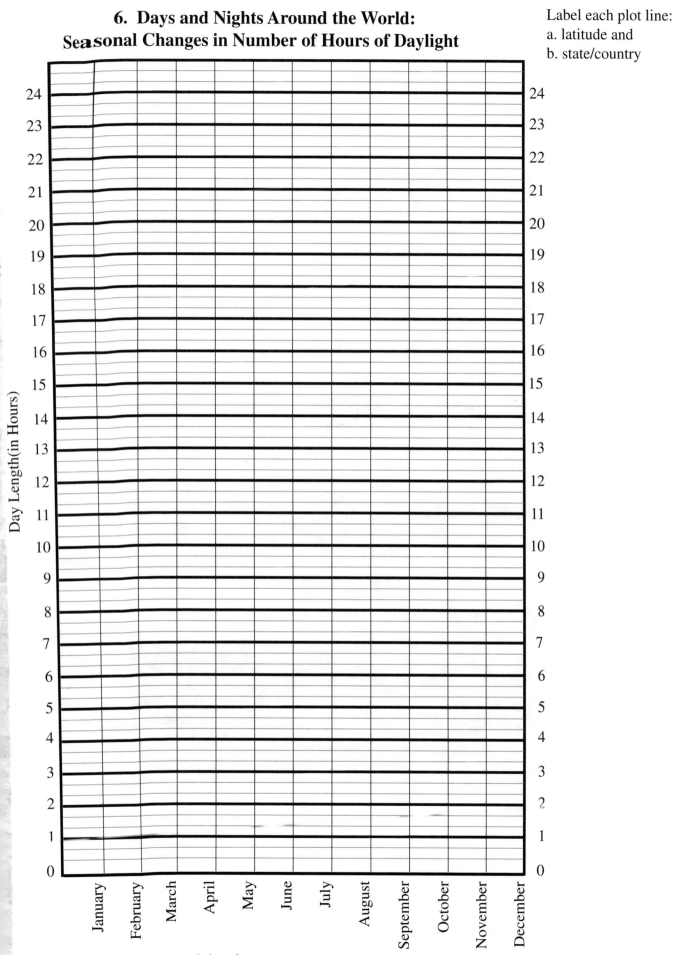

Day Length(in Hours)

The Real Reasons for Seasons: Sun-Earth Connections
A Great Explorations in Math and Science (GEMS) Teacher's Guide

*Can you explain
The reasons why
The seasons come
And then pass by?*

Lawrence Hall of Science   University of California at Berkeley